The American Pullman Cars of the Midland Railway

J. B. Radford C. Eng., M. I. Mech. E.

LONDON

IAN ALLAN LTD

To my wife Jo

George Mortimer Pullman (1831-1897).
Courtesy The Pullman Company

First published 1984

ISBN 0 7110 1387 X

© Ian Allan Ltd 1984

Published by Ian Allan Ltd, Shepperton, Surrey;
and printed by Ian Allan Printing Ltd at their works
at Coombelands in Runnymede, England.

Contents

Front endpaper:
Interior of a Pullman sleeping car arranged for day-time use, with the bunks neatly raised up out of the way in the roof corners.
Crown Copyright Midland Railway Official photograph courtesy National Railway Museum

Rear endpaper:
Sumptuously fitted out interior of the first-class non-smoking saloon in the 1900 Pullman sleeping cars of the Midland Railway.
Crown Copyright Midland Railway Official photograph courtesy National Railway Museum

Foreword and acknowledgements

The arrival of the American Pullman cars on the Midland Railway heralded a new era in coaching stock standards and the competition which they engendered acted as a springboard from which great improvements came on Britain's railways as a whole.

George Behrend has told the story of how Pullman and his cars arrived upon the European scene, and the events which followed right up to 1960, in his excellent book *Pullman in Europe*, but to date no work has appeared dedicated solely to the Pullmans of the Midland Railway and the Pullman workshops at Derby where the kits of parts, delivered from the Pullman shops in Detroit, were assembled, maintained and rebuilt, which is the gap that this work is designed to fill.

I have drawn freely upon the official records of the Midland Railway and the Great Northern Railway which are now deposited in the Public Records Office at Kew, augmented by other information from official sources, the Stretton papers in the Leicester Libraries and information from Behrend's book mentioned above. This has been supplemented by material from various magazine articles, personal correspondence and other miscellaneous data.

For illustrative material I have to thank the National Railway Museum for supplying prints from the official Midland Railway and other negatives now deposited with them together with many friends and other correspondents including David Tee, R. G. Jarvis, the Historical Model Railway Society, George Dow, and R. H. Offord who also supplied the drawing of the lettering and numbering on the oval plaques on the side of the original sleeping car 'Midland', the body of which is thankfully preserved along with those of an example of each of the two day car types, at the Midland Railway Centre, Butterley, Derbyshire.

I would welcome any additional information whatever relating to these cars, especially photographs, which will throw further light on the subject and which could possibly be included in any future revision of this work.

Brian Radford
Allestree
Derby
June 1983

4

1 Pullman's Early History

It was the assassination of President Abraham Lincoln of the United States of America that gave George Mortimer Pullman a unique and unrepeatable opportunity to bring his revolutionary ideas before a wide public audience. When the body of the slain President arrived in Chicago by rail on its way to Springfield the state officials looked round for the most splendid conveyance possible to carry Lincoln's widow on the final stage of her journey. What could be better than 'Pioneer', Pullman's first sleeping car? Tradition has it that she herself requested its use having seen it on a visit to Illinois early in 1865 and been entranced by it.

Built at a cost of over $20,000, five times more than any previous sleeping car, with a floor covered with rich red carpet, the seats covered with brocaded fabrics, the doorframes of highly polished choice woods and the berths panelled with ornamented wood the whole lit by silver-trimmed oil lamps and hung with gilt edged mirrors, during building it had been christened 'Pullman's Folly', but at its unveiling it was hailed 'as the wonder of the age'.

It was, however, too wide to pass any of the existing station platforms, and no railroad company would have anything to do with it — until the Presidential emergency that is! Platforms along the intended route were hurriedly widened and the dead President's widow climbed aboard 'Pioneer' which was everywhere received with an outpouring of acclaim and publicity that exceeded George Pullman's wildest dreams.

From that day onward Pullmans' name became a household word and his cars became widely accepted. The Chicago & Alton Railroad hired the 'Pioneer' on Pullman's terms and placed it in service, and he began building more cars for other railroads until by the end of 1866 he had 48 cars in service.

On 22 February 1867 the Pullman Palace Car Company was incorporated and by the end of that decade George Pullman dominated the sleeping car business of the entire United States of America.

George Mortimer Pullman himself was born in Brocton, Chautauqua County, New York State on 3 March 1831. His father was a general mechanic and George was the third of an eventual 10 children. At the age of 14 he began earning money by working in a farm supplies store and in 1848, at the age of 17, he joined his elder brother, a cabinet maker in Albion, New York State.

During his travels selling his brother's cabinents he made a journey in 1853 from Buffalo to Westfield, during which he travelled in a sort of sleeping car. It was in fact no more than a couchette and the 58-mile trip was passed in some discomfort, there being no heating of any kind and the only illumination available was from candles. There were no sheets, blankets or pillows and he slept on a rough mattress fully clothed. This sleeping car was merely an ordinary coach with a few crude extras. Three wooden shelves were permanently fixed to the sides in a tier arrangement so that the vehicle could not be used for day travel. Passengers wishing to avail themselves of the facilities merely climbed fully dressed on to one of the shelves!

Pullman decided as a result of this experience that travellers overnight would be quite willing to pay for extra comforts, and began measuring and sketching out his ideas for converting a normal day car into a better class of sleeping car with comfortable bedding and plush upholstery. Everyone knew the problem, but what was lacking was the knowhow.

In 1858 he obtained the consent of the Chicago & Alton Railroad, a line extending some 280 miles from Chicago to St Louis, to convert two of that company's coaches at their Bloomington shops so that facing seats could be made into one berth for nightime use and an upper berth lowered from the roof on pulleys could provide a berth for the second traveller. A primitive washroom with a tin basin and jug was provided at each end of the vehicles. Also provided were oil lamps and box stores and the total cost was $1,000 per car.

The vehicles in question, numbered 9 and 10 were 44ft long in the body and 49ft 9in overall and the internal width was 8ft 11in.

When the first car, number 9, went into service on 1 September 1859, the original conductor was 22-year-old J. L. Barnes and he remembers the event as being rather uneventful. There was no crowd, business was rather poor in the early days of the service, and he remembers passengers being reluctant to take off their boots before getting into their berths for the night. He did not think that many slept much during the journey. From Bloomington to Chicago, Barnes remarked to Pullman that it was a fine car to which the latter briefly replied: 'It ought to be. It cost enough'.

On this car and its sister number 10 Pullman first introduced the 'Pullman Supplement' for the privilege of sleeping in his cars, in this case $2. It is interesting to note that the railway owned older cars of the Michigan Railroad and charged $1.50 for use, it being thought that $2 was more than the public would pay, but on mixing their own and Pullman's sleepers, it was the latter that the public clamoured to sleep in.

After a few trips it was decided to dispense with Barnes' services as Pullman conductor, and the car was put in the care of the train's general conductor.

There was then a hiatus for a few years during which Pullman became a contractor specialising in the removal of buildings by jacking them up and moving them in one piece. His work took him to Chicago where a four storey brick building, the Tremont House Hotel, was threatened with demolition owing to its low position and trouble with its drains. The building was jacked up and new foundations provided, and Pullman gained some notoriety locally through this operation which was achieved without breaking a pane of glass, spilling a drop of beer or causing chambermaids to break a single piece of crockery.

In 1862, with the Civil War raging and passenger travel falling off, Pullman went west to Colorado, where he engaged himself in trading and mining being involved in the gold rush camp called 'Pike's Peak or Bust', but in 1863 he returned to Chicago with capital of $20,000 after disposing of his business interests, and turned his attention yet again to the business of sleeping cars.

In 1864 he undertook the construction of the first car built entirely to his own designs, the erection of which was done in an old repair shed belonging to the Chicago

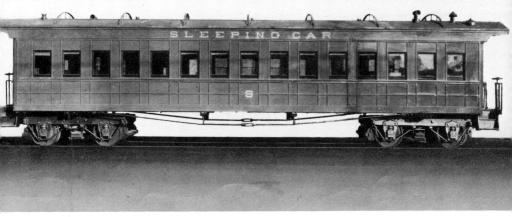

Above:

Exterior of Pullman's first conversion to a sleeping car — the Chicago & Alton Railway No 9 which was tried out along with a similar car, No 10.
Courtesy The Pullman Company

Below left:

Interior of prototype sleeping car No 9 on the Chicago & Alton Railroad showing the convertible seating arrangement. *Courtesy The Pullman Company*

Below right:

Interior of prototype sleeping car No 9 on the Chicago & Alton Railroad showing the convertible seating arranged for sleeping accommodation.
Courtesy The Pullman Company

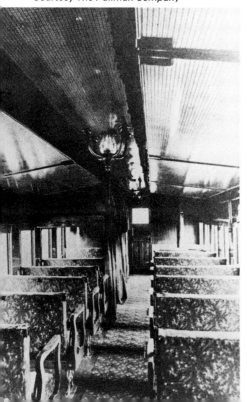

& Alton Railroad. The work occupied more than a year and 'far exceeded all prior experiments in luxury and practicability', being what some would call the 'unlucky 13th' vehicle incorporating Pullman's ideas. He was assisted by Leonard Siebert, a mechanic on the Alton line, whom he hired to help in the huge task.

Costing $18,239.31c without equipment, and with a total cost of $20,178.14c completed, this was the first real Pullman car proper and was duly named 'Pioneer'. It incorporated Pullman's by now perfected swinging berths which were raised to fit up against the roof when not in use, the lower bunk for sleeping purposes being produced by adapting the day seats, which faced each other in pairs, into a comfortable bed. Pure linen bedding was provided. Heating was by means of grilles fed with hot air from a furnace beneath the floor and lighting was by candle power, although these were set in elaborate chandeliers. The interior finish was in polished black walnut and washstands of marble were provided in the lavatory compartment. The floor was covered with rich red carpet, the seats upholstered with brocaded fabrics and the walls were hung with gilt-edged mirrors.

The hinged upper berth and the hinged back and seat cushion which formed the lower berth were the subject of separate patents applied for in 1864 and granted to Pullman and a boyhood friend, Ben Field of Albion, New York, whom he took into partnership.

'Pioneer' was provided with two four wheeled bogies, having much improved springing and solid rubber shock absorbers. However, it was one foot higher and 2ft 6in wider than any other car in service and therefore, would not clear the then loading gauge for the line. In consequence after completion in the autumn of 1864 it lay out of use in the Chicago shed for almost a year and became known as 'Pullman's Folly'. 'Never before' wrote Joseph Husband 'had such a car been seen; never had the wildest flights of fancy imagined such magnificence'.

Pullman was a very religious man, left money to churches and built seminaries and, although ruthless, was nevertheless a lover of beautiful things.

President Lincoln's assassination on 14 April 1865 occasioned the eventual use of the car as recounted earlier, coupled with the fact that Mrs Lincoln was taken ill on the way to Chicago with her husband's body and upon arrival there Pullman offered her the use of the car. The Chicago & Alton line altered its station platforms forthwith in haste and on 2 May 1865 'Pioneer' made its historic first journey.

By 1867, the year incidentally in which he introduced 'coloured porters' (as Negro Pullman attendants were always called in America), Pullman had a fleet of some 48 cars operating although some of the companies showed a remarkable reluctance in accepting the new comfort standards brought before the public in the new vehicles. The coloured porters were little more than emancipated slaves being expected to travel long distances, during which they received no payment of any kind, in order to book on for a further paid duty roster. In that year (1867) the Pullman Palace Car Company was formed by incorporation on 22 February with a capital of $100,000, and in 1870 acquired its first car building plant at Detroit, Michigan. However, a further 300 cars had to be assembled by other builders and railroad's shops before his new works became fully established and able to cope with by now large public demand for his cars.

Another aspect of Pullman's business was hotel or dining cars, and he produced the first hotel car, which was named 'President', for the Great Western Railway of Canada

Above:
'Pullman's Folly' — his original sleeping car 'Pioneer' built at his own expense and which incorporated his latest ideas for converting a day car for night-time use.
Courtesy The Pullman Company

Below:
Interior view of 'Pioneer' showing the convertible day seats used as beds at night and the upper berths stowed away out of use above the windows at each side.
Courtesy The Pullman Company

in 1867. This combined sleeping space with excellent dining facilities offering a dish of steak and potatoes for sixty cents or a plate of sugar-cured ham for forty cents. Two more, 'Western World' and 'Kalamazoo', were built and the three placed in service between Chicago and Buffalo over the Michigan Central and Great Western of Canada route. On 8 April 1867 'Western World' left Chicago with an excursion party and ran all the way to Utica.

Pullman married Hattie Sanger of Chicago on 13 June 1867, by whom he had four children.

The following year Pullman introduced his first purpose-built full length dining car 'Delmonico', named after a famous New York Swiss restaurateur, and ran it on the Chicago & Alton Railroad. It quickly proved a great attraction and Pullman added train catering as part of his activities, whilst all over the United States other railroad companies hastened to set up their own dining car operations.

F. S. Williams makes some references to travel in American Pullman cars in the fifth edition of his valuable work *Our Iron Roads*, which appeared in 1884, as follows:

'Some of the sleeping cars on American lines appear to have their drawbacks. A traveller tells us of his experiences in one of them. "There was something touching," he says, "in the perfect neatness and comfort of the beds. In the midst of a great, dirty, roaring, selfish city, one could hardly have looked for such domesticity and motherly providence. How cool and fresh the linen looked. How springy the mattresses! How soft the pillows! Surely this must be the happiest way to bridge the two hundred and odd miles between New York and Boston. To sleep, and, by a sleep, to say we end the newsboys and pop-corn man, urchin with gum-drops, and with Ridley's candies, the long array of 'bound books', novels, 'Harper's', 'Leslies', 'Fun for Three Months' and, though last not least, the stench, the gloom, the smoke, the dirt, of that foul place, the depôt at New Haven! 'Tis a consummation devoutly to be wished! I little thought that in that sleep there might be dreams!.

' "After the tedious gentleman had given me my ticket, I suffered myself to be led like a lamb to a bench in an alcove at one side of the car. This bench a youth shared with me, and opposite were two other victims. All four of us were innocent and unsuspecting; we entered into a light and courteous conversation; we played about the subect that lay nearest to our thoughts, as though we were utterly indifferent to it; we encouraged each other in a fatuous confidence in the honour and good intentions of those to whom he had blindly entrused ourselves. We expressed our belief in the beds! Each one told the other that he expected to sleep like a top! We believed we should, or we tried to believe it; and as we really knew nothing about tops and how they sleep, perhaps we did sleep like them. In that case, tops are a miserable class of creatures. Conversation soon became confidential. The youth, my neighbour, wound up his watch. He said that he had been told that he must particularly look out for pickpockets in the sleeping cars! His papa had told him that they looked remarkably like gentlemen. His watch was a valuable one. He had more money on him than he cared to lose. His aunt had advised him to pin it into his fob; but his brother had told him that all such devices were useless against pickpockets.

' "Then the man appeared who makes up the beds. He pulled levers up and down, shot bolts, turned windlasses, adjusted screws, and finally we saw our snug alcoves transformed into four beds of such a guileless and prepossessing appearance as might

10

have deceived the very elect! For us, as for the rest, snow-white sheets were spread, crimson blankets — which the chilly August air, and the dreary, pattering rain made seem most comfortable — were cosily tucked in, plumpest pillows invited our heads, and the shadowing curtains enclosed me and the confiding youth in their folds while we undressed for the night. But, reader, I am no poet, and cannot describe that night.

' "After a few hours of abortive attempts at sleeping, I at last found myself, in the early grey of morning, as wide awake as if it were broad noon. I leaned out of my coffin and looked about in the dim light to see how it fared with the other dead people. My confiding friend was sitting on a pillow on the floor by the side of his berth, apparently wondering why his maiden-aunt had not included sleeping-cars in her list of dangers he was to avoid." '

Commenting on the general spread of the Pullman cars in America and even beyond it is worth recording that whilst in 1867 there were only thirty-seven of them in America, five years later there were 700 in remunerative operation; and the company's contracts were with more than 150 different railways, and extended over 30,000 miles of American railway.

To close the chapter on the general subject of Pullman travel, Williams makes the following somewhat humorous allusions:

'One of the effects, we will not say advantages, of travelling in a long car may be to promote sociability. "An American," says a St Louis paper, in an article on native politeness, "may not be so elegant at a dinner party, but he will not ride half a day in a railway car without speaking to the fellow-passenger at his elbow, as the Englishman will." "No," remarks an American critic, "indeed he will not: fore George he will not. How often, oh, how often, have we wished that he would! But he won't. He will pounce upon a stranger whom he has never seen before in all his life, and talk him deaf, dumb and blind in fifty miles. Catch an American holding his mouth shut when he has a chance to talk to some man who doesn't want to be talked to." '

But sociability in Pullman cars may, especially under certain circumstances, take more demonstrative forms. 'I have never,' observes another traveller, 'got so well acquainted with the passengers on the train as I did the other day on the Milwaukee & St Paul Railroad. We were going at the rate of about 30 miles an hour, and another train from the other direction telescoped us. We were all thrown into each other's society, and brought into immediate social contact, so to speak. I went over and sat in the lap of a corpulent lady from Manitoba, and a girl from Chicago jumped over nine seats and sat down on the plug hat of a preacher from La Crosse, with so much timid, girlish enthusiasm that it shoved his hat clear down over his shoulders. Everybody seemed to lay aside the usual cool reserve of strangers, and we made ourselves entirely at home. A shy young man, with an emaciated oil-cloth valise, left his own seat and went over and sat down in a lunch basket, where a bridal couple seemed to be wrestling with their first picnic. Do you suppose that reticent young man would have done such a thing on ordinary occasions? Do you think if he had been at a celebration at home that he would have risen impetuously and gone where those people were eating by themselves, and sat down in the cranberry jelly of a total stranger? I should rather think not. Why, one old man, who probably at home led the class-meeting, and who was as dignified as

Roscoe Conkling's father, was eating a piece of custard pie when we met the other train, and he left his own seat and went over to the other end of the car and shot the piece of custard pie into the ear of a beautiful widow from Iowa. People travelling somehow forget the austerity of their home lives, and form acquaintances that sometimes last through life.'

Above:
An artist's impression of an early American Pullman at night.

Above right:
An artist's impression of an early American Pullman during the day.

Below:
A Victorian outing to Blackpool is in prospect for this group assembled on the platform at Carlisle in 1899 in front of their special excursion train which includes two Pullman cars in its formation. The leading vehicle is a dining saloon, either 'Delmonico' or 'Windsor' whilst the one on the right is one of the former 1st/2nd day cars which were converted to dining saloons Nos 16, 17 and 18 in 1884.
Miss M. N. Burgess courtesy D. F. Tee

2 Midland Initiative

By 1872 as we have seen in the previous chapter, the United States of America had a positive lead in both the design and comfort of its trains, and George Pullman had extended his influence to most of the major railroad companies, bringing luxurious palatial accommodation for both the day and night-time traveller alike, pandering to his every whim in return for a modest supplement.

In stark contrast the passenger accommodation in Britain, birthplace of the railways, had hardly been improved from the pioneer days, and four and six wheeled coaches were still the order of the day with half partitioned open carriages and plain wooden seats being the best afforded to the lowly third class traveller. All luggage was still carried on the roofs of carriages, and James Joseph Allport, General Manager of the Midland Railway commented 'I have felt saddened to see third class passengers shunted on to a siding in cold, and bitter weather — a train containing amongst others lightly-clad women and children — for the convenience of allowing the more comfortable and warmly clad passengers (travelling first and second class) to pass them. I have even known third class trains to be shunted into a siding to allow express goods to pass'.

Allport resolved to improve things at least so far as his own company was concerned and in the autumn of 1872, he paid a visit to America to see the improvements there, which he had read of, at first hand. He was granted special leave of absence by the Midland Board of Directors and followed Nagelmackers to the States, but not before his Board had decreed that, as from 1 April 1872 third class passengers should be admitted to all Midland trains, a decision which outraged some of the Midlands' competitors. Allport travelled some 6,000 miles across the American railroad network, much of the time in Pullman's impressive parlour and sleeping cars. He was captivated not only by the comfort and the smooth riding of the vehicles on bogies (unlike their British six and four-wheeled counterparts!), but by the public's keenness to utilise these facilities extensively wherever they were to be found.

Upon his return he brought up the matter of the Pullman cars and on 5 November 1872 the Midland Traffic Committee discussed the whole question of providing these vehicles for special trains, referring any decision to the Board. Allport persuaded the Midland Directors to receive Pullman and to present him and his proposals, with plans and models, before the half-yearly shareholders meeting to be held on 15 February 1873. The meeting was first given details of George Pullman's history and all about his cars and their new standards of comfort, and were then told that he himself was present, which announcement was received with cheers from some quarters. Sceptics were disarmed by Pullman's offer, at his own risk, to build cars equal to a first class hotel and constructed to suit the English loading gauge, to ship them to England and to meet all the costs of their operation in return for permission to charge his 'Pullman Supplement' on top of the normal fare. Cars were to be supplied complete with his own attendants as demand warranted, but he was to have exclusive rights to provide these services involving sleeping, dining and parlour cars for a period of 15 years.

This proposal was agreed to with the proviso that Pullman should design and build carriages having the same Pullman outline, but providing non-supplementary accommodation for all three classes of passenger. These vehicles were always to be provided as part of a rake of Pullman vehicles in a train and were to be purchased outright by the Midland on completion.

The agreement with Pullman was signed on 18 February 1873 and by the end of the year crates of parts for the vehicles, which were to be supplied from the Detroit workshops of the Pullman Palace Car Company in knocked-down condition, were arriving at Derby, headquarters of the Midland Company, for re-assembly and commissioning.

At the same meeting of the Traffic Committee it was resolved that one van and one carriage be built for each train to the same basic sizes and construction as the Pullman cars and these were eventually built as four third class brake/baggage cars and four first/second class composite cars to be described later.

On 20 May the same committee considered a sketch of sheds which would be required at Derby for the accommodation of the Pullman Palace Cars and, it having been explained that a portion of the cars already under construction in America would

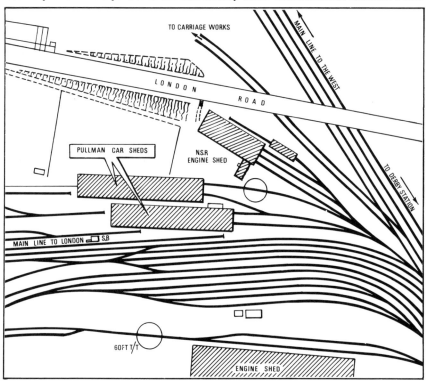

be ready for delivery in June, it was resolved that the plan be referred to the Way and Works Committee with a view to a shed of sufficient capacity to accommodate half of the cars being provided by the time named, the site to be fixed by the officers.

By 2 December, 1873 cars were already being erected in sheds alongside the London Road at Derby and adjacent to the North Staffordshire Railway locomotive depot, and the Traffic Committee resolved that the ends of this shed be boarded up and alterations made in the roof lights to improve lighting in the place. On 17 November of the following year an even greater step forward was made when it was resolved that the Locomotive Committee be requested to have the wooden shed used by the Pullman Company fitted up with gas.

By 21 January 1874 the first sleeping car, named 'Midland' had been completed and was ready for trial running. This car was 58ft 9in long overall and the body was 51ft 8½in long and 8ft 9in wide over the mouldings. It had end observation platforms 8ft wide by 2ft 10in long, having wrought iron gates at the sides and end railings. The roof of clerestory type, with swept down, curved and domed ends, continued beyond the body proper to partially cover the open platform at each end.

The bogies were of the American type, but with Mansell pattern wooden wheels 3ft 6in in diameter, which was larger than the standard in the States. Most of the bogie was of wooden construction with ironwork bolted on to the main wooden framings, and the bogies were set 36ft 9in apart.

Inside 'Midland' the main saloon had 10 sofa sections which comprised pairs of longitudinal seats facing each other each capable of comfortably seating two passengers during daytime use. Beyond this were two private state-rooms each having a sofa section below the window and a pair of single seats which could be turned to face each other and the seat squab pulled out allowing part of the seat back to fall, thus providing a further berth for night-time use. The sofa seat squabs could be similarly pulled out towards the centre of the car, allowing part of the back again to fall to provide a lower sleeping berth. The upper berths, normally raised out of sight up against the roof corners, could be lowered on pulleys for night-time use, being hinged at the body side.

At the state room end of 'Midland' a ladies toilet and water closet was provided at one side and a Baker solid fuel heating stove in a recess at the other. The gentlemen's toilet and water closet were installed each side of the gangway at the other end of the car beyond the saloon. Water for the toilets was raised from low level tanks below the floor.

The windows, which comprised one large and two small ones for each sofa section length, could only be opened upwards, due to the trussing of the vehicle below the window level, and were each fitted with roller blinds.

British carriages of the time rested upon a separate underframe, but Pullmans were entirely different, having a heavily built trussed side framing below the windows within the body side, strengthened underneath by iron truss rods with adjustable barrel nuts to set the correct camber. The solebars consisted of Oregon pine of 7in by 6in section, and this made for a very substantial construction when coupled with metal tie-bars used vertically to connect the solebar with the cantrail member.

Interior lighting was by means of 'Argand' kerosene lamps suspended from the centre of the clerestory roof, and was of course far superior to the then standard English illumination which comprised pot oil lamps inserted from the outside of the

15

carriage through holes in the ceiling and which burned rape oil.

Also superior was the heating of the Pullman car by means of the Baker coke-fired, coiled tube boiler which supplied hot water through closed circuit hot water pipes fed from a hot water tank mounted beside the clerestory and which fed the radiators via the piping circuit on a feed and return system. At that time of course, British carriages relied almost exclusively on flat pot footwarmers which were supplied by platform staff on request, but which frequently were either too hot to touch, or too cold to be of any benefit to the traveller.

A contemporary description of the various cars which appeared in the *Derby Mercury* for 28 January 1874 is appended below.

'The Pullman cars on the Midland Railway

'One of the results of the recent visit of Mr Allport, General Manager of the Midland Railway Company, to Canada and the United States, was an arrangement by which the celebrated Pullman Palace Cars are to be placed within the reach of travellers on the Midland line. This luxurious carriage owes its origin to the gentleman whose name it bears, and who was led to contrive the means for making the long journeys across the American continent less wearying to travellers. Ten years ago Mr Longstreet, who is now erecting similar cars at the Midland Railway station in this town, built the first and now there are between six and seven hundred travelling on the railways in the United States. The ingenious contrivances by which a carriage full of seats is turned into a sleeping car are the subject of patents, and these are now the property of the Pullman Car Company, which owns all the existing carriages of this nature. This Company has entered into an arrangement with the directors of the Midland Railway to run 16 carriages on their line charging passengers a fixed tariff for their use, in addition to the ordinary fare. Three of these carriages are now near completion at the Midland Railway Station, Derby. The whole of the work has been done in the United States, and brought over here to be put together.

'The cars are 50ft in length, with the entrance at each end, and a passage direct through them, down the centre. They run on two trucks, which are square frames with double pairs of wheels, and are fixed at each end of the car, upon a pivot on which they turn, so that the double pairs of wheels adjust themselves readily to a curve, just as the fore wheels of an ordinary carriage, and there is less danger of their leaving the rails. They rest on a double set of springs, elliptical springs at right angles to the rails, and four circular coiled springs, one at each angle. The cars are strengthened with iron trusses. The exterior appearance is handsome and striking. It is however inside that the special features of the Pullman cars are presented. They are of two kinds, Day or Parlour Cars, and Sleeping Cars. The former are fitted with two rows of handsome easy chairs, covered with crimson velvet, between which the passage extends. These are fixed on silver-plated pivots, so that the traveller can turn round easily, and face his fellow passengers. The Sleeping Cars are adapted both for day and night. By day they present handsome double seats, facing each other at right angles to and on each side of the passage. To turn these into beds there is an ingenious contrivance by which the opposite seats are brought forward so as to cover the space between them, and the backs are lowered, and thus the whole forms an enclosure in which two persons may lie. Just above a graceful curve covers during the day a place for stowing the bed clothes, and when the front is lowered an upper tier of beds is formed, each of which is

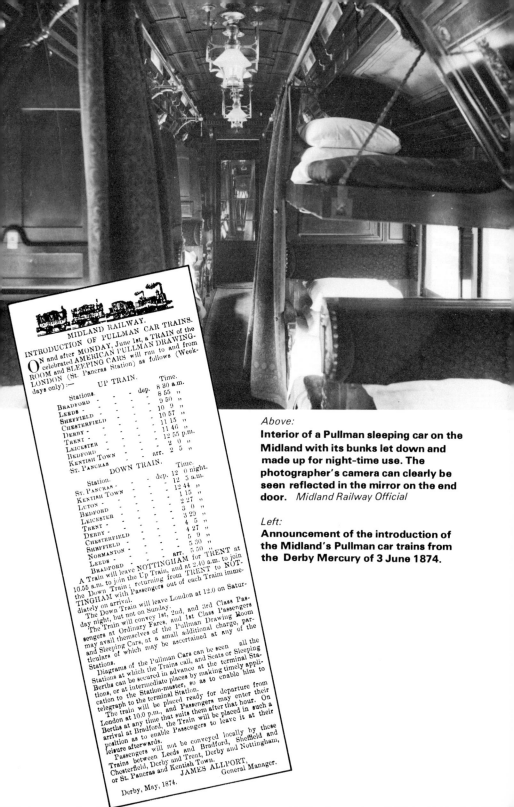

Above:

Interior of a Pullman sleeping car on the Midland with its bunks let down and made up for night-time use. The photographer's camera can clearly be seen reflected in the mirror on the end door. *Midland Railway Official*

Left:

Announcement of the introduction of the Midland's Pullman car trains from the Derby Mercury of 3 June 1874.

ample for a single person. In each class of car there is at the end a warming apparatus. A coil of pipes passes around a fire, and these being filled with water it is heated and constantly circulates under the seats occupied by the passengers. In each of the cars there are two private apartments, one of which will accommodate five persons, or which may be thrown together for a larger family or party. In the day cars each of these contains two arm chairs and a couch; in the sleeping cars the seats can easily be turned into beds. There are ladies' and gentlemen's retiring rooms, with every convenience, and a supply of water for drinking, and hot water for washing. Some of the American cars for the longest journeys are supplied with cooking kitchens. The interior fittings of the carriages are exceedingly elegant. They are of American black walnut, polished, with panels and other parts veneered with French knotted walnut or burl, and figured decorations in gold are employed with good effect. Almost the whole of the metal fittings, except the lamp frames, are silver-plated, the floors are covered with Wilton carpets and everything is graceful and handsome, whilst considerable ingenuity is displayed in every part of the construction. The provision for ventilation is very complete, and under perfect control. The ventilators are double, one opens towards the front, and by the motion of the train secures the entrance of a current of fresh air into the car, the other opens to the rear, and serves as a means of exhausting the air from it. They are opened or closed independently, and can be adjusted to any degree desired. The cars being the property of the Pullman Car Company, the charge for their use will be an addition to the ordinary fare. In the United States, reducing the amounts to English money, the extra charge for the Parlour Cars is for 50 miles two shillings (10p); for 100 miles three shillings (15p); and for 400 miles four shillings (20p). The sleeping cars are charged eight shillings (40p) a night for a double berth, which would hold two persons, though one would be more comfortable. For the journey from New York to Chicago, a distance of 1,000 miles, and which occupies two nights and a day, the charge for the use of the Sleeping Car, in addition to the ordinary fare, is five dollars, or £1. As the English railways are narrower than those in the United States, the seats are three inches narrower on each side in these English cars, being three feet instead of three feet three inches. Besides the increased comfort, these carriages must be very favourable to conversation. People can walk erect along the passage and can look out and breathe the air at the ends as well as by the windows.

'Mr Longstreet is also erecting for the Midland Company several cars on the model of those ordinarily used in the United States, for first, second, and third class passengers. These are of the same length as the Pullman cars, 50ft, with a passage down the centre and seats on each side.* The advantage of these cars have often been noticed. There is a complete communication between all parts of the train. The carriages are connected by a self-locking apparatus, and they can be separated with ease, without descending from the carriage, so that there is no coupling nor uncoupling. The small platforms at the end by which the carriages are entered come within a few inches of each other, and it is easy to step from one carriage to the next, and in this way the conductor traverses the whole train. As there are only two entrances for a large car, no doubt egress will be rather slower, but there will be less danger of

---

*The description given here is at variance with that given later in the text which is based on the observations of Monsieur Banderali in August 1874 who described the 1st/2nd class cars as of the corridor type. The surviving body at the Midland Railway Centre appears to confirm his description which has been used to reconstruct the internal layout shown in the diagram in Appendix 5.

passengers suffering from accidents by getting out before the train stops. The third class trains will have divisions at each end, appropriated to passengers' luggage, or, as the Americans call it, baggage. We believe the Midland Company is disposed to try on these trains the American plan of checking luggage, by which passengers entrust their luggage before starting to an officer of the company, receiving for each article a check corresponding in number with one placed upon it.'

By 20 January 1874 James Allport was able to report that the Pullman cars had been tried on every portion of the line except the part between Ambergate and Leeds. The road bridges and tunnels had been found to be of sufficient width to admit of their passing each other with the exception of Marple Tunnel. It was recommended that this be altered, Allport stating that the engineer of the Manchester Sheffield & Lincolnshire Railway Company had estimated that the necessary alterations would cost £23,000. It was resolved that, as this part of the line belonged to the Sheffield & Midland Joint Committee, it be referred to that Committee with authority given to the Midland Directors composing it to agree to any arrangement which they considered to be in the best interests of the Company.

On 15 February 1874 the second sleeping car 'Excelsior' emerged from the Derby shops and on 17 March the two left Derby in the charge of Kirtley 2-4-0 No 906, whose tender had been specially fitted with the Miller automatic centre coupling to suit that on the Pullmans', on a first trip to London for the benefit of 'officials of the line'. The journey was completed in $2\frac{1}{2}$hrs with two stops of 3min each, and clearly everyone was delighted with the outcome.

Four days later on 21 March, the two sleeping cars were supplemented by the first parlour car, 'Victoria' on a public demonstration run from St Pancras to Bedford and back with some 80 persons on board. Luncheon was served during the trip, the first ever meal provided on a British train, the caterers being Messrs Speirs and Pond, who it was noted 'had come from Melbourne to improve our railway refreshment facilities'.

'The visitors to Bedford were asked to write their names in a book' wrote a deeply impressed journalist of the time (*The Times*, 23 March 1874), 'and they did so without the smallest difficulty when the train was running at the rate of 50 miles an hour'. Clearly the occasion was an impressive introduction to what was to follow.

The first parlour car 'Victoria', used on this train, was an historic vehicle, for no other such Pullmans had been tried out before either in Britain or the United States. Its airy saloon was fitted with 17 individual armchairs mounted on a pivot so that each could be revolved to face in any direction and also tilted backwards if required. Upholstery was moquette with a floral pattern, some of the chair backs being buttoned and others plain.

Beyond the open saloon, and served from a side corridor, were two private rooms each containing two chairs and a cross sofa seating five passengers in all. At this end of the car was the usual Baker solid fuel-fired heating stove in its own compartment whilst at the other end at the sides of the short corridor leading to the end platform were separate ladies' and gentlemen's lavatory compartments.

The overall length of the body was 51ft 6in and length over the end platforms 58ft according to the lithograph, and two four wheeled bogies on a 6ft 6in wheelbase were pitched at 39ft centres. Overall height of the vehicle from rail was 12ft 11in and overall width 8ft 9in. The total cost of the vehicle was over £3,000.

19

A passage from F. S. Williams *Our Iron Roads* 5th edition, published in 1884, is worthy of quoting in full respecting the first trip.

'When the first journey of the Pullman train was run, it was from St Pancras to Bedford. "Literally nothing," wrote one who then travelled, "seemed left to desire. Entering the train from one end, you were introduced to the parlour car, a luxurious contrivance for short lines and day-travel only. It was a tastefully and richly decorated saloon, over fifty feet long, light, warm, well ventilated, and exquisitely carpeted, upholstered and furnished. Along each side, and close to the windows, were crimson-cushioned easy chairs, in which, by means of a pivot, you might swing yourself round to converse with your neighbour, or, by means of one of the thousand ingenious contrivances with which the whole train abounded, you might tilt yourself back to the proper angle of enjoyment. The centre is free for passing to and fro. There are various little saloons of the private box order, in which a family party might make themselves happy. Then you came to the drawing-room sleeping car, another long, well-appointed saloon, with fixed seats at the windows like short sofas, two and two, and facing each other. Between them a firm, convenient table could be planted, and upon one of them we were able, while the train ran at over fifty miles an hour, to write without difficulty. The tables removed, the seats lowered to meet each other became an admirable bedstead, while some beautifully ornamented and finished panels overhead, that appeared to be merely part of the sloping roof of the saloon, were unfastened, and in a moment converted into equally comfortable upper berths. By-and-by the saloon was restored to its normal drawing-room aspect, the tables were again put up, waiters entered with snow-white cloths, pantries and anterooms were brought into operation, and there appeared a dining hall as complete in its requirements as the drawing-room and sleeping-room had been in theirs."

'How far the Pullman car will be generally preferred in England is a matter of some doubt. Americans themselves when they come to this country, appear well content with the matchless speed of English railway travelling and the comfort of half-filled ordinary first-class carriages. When Lord George Bentinck said on an off-day at Newmarket, only a few owners, trainers, and jockeys being present, "This is what I like; I hate a crowd", he expressed a feeling widely distributed among our poulation, and one adverse to the adoption of long cars. They are, without question, a great boon to ladies and to solitary travellers. Relieved of the custody of her impedimenta, of all fear of insult, and pleased with the handsome surroundings of the Pullman drawing-room, the lady traveller will appreciate the provision made for her comfort; and the more social varieties of the Englishman if travelling alone, may also take kindly to the long car. A shy and sensitive minority will perhaps prefer the comparative seclusion of the ordinary first-class carriage.'

Sir Edward Baines is recorded as observing that the Pullmans were 'fit for the journeyings of monarchs', a tribute indeed!

Back in Committee the question of fitting up the Midlands' own day cars to run with the Pullmans was raised by the Traffic Committee on 17 March and it was resolved that the Carriage & Wagon Committee be requested to arrange for the upholstering of the carriages to be done by the (Midland) company. This was done, the first class accommodation being trimmed in blue cloth, the second class in green and the third class in red.

A proposed timetable for the first Pullman car train service to run between London and Bradford was approved by the Traffic Committee on 19 May 1874 to commence on 1 June and be carried out for one month.

The service duly commenced on the date arranged with a five car rake behind the engine comprising a third class baggage car, a first/second composite (both of these being Midland day cars), a sleeping car, a parlour car and a further third class baggage car in the rear. This gave accommodation for 200 persons in a train weighing some 100 tons.

This first service left Bradford for London (St Pancras) at 8.30am reaching London at 2.05pm and returned from St Pancras as a sleeping car service at midnight, passengers being allowed to occupy their berths from 10pm and remain there until 8am the following morning (despite arriving in Bradford at 5.50am), giving half an hour for the train to be cleaned and serviced before the start of the second journey.

A report in the *Railway Fly Sheet* for June 1874, remarks upon the 'pleasant, quiet journey' of this first service trip and told of a rubber of whist played comfortably and with hushed voices during the trip, the inference being that such an entertainment carried out in relative peace and quiet was not possible in the ordinary stock of the period.

From July the midnight Pullman sleeping car express to Bradford was retimed to leave at 11.50pm while the 8.30am Pullman car express Bradford to London left at 9.20am to run direct via Erewash Valley and was accelerated to arrive St Pancras at 2.35pm. According to Ahrons these Bradford-London trains ran at first via Derby.

Later in the summer the rake was strengthened by the addition of a second sleeping car. The supplement charged varied according to the distance travelled by day from one shilling (5p) to five shillings (25p) whilst the charge for a sleeping berth for any distance was six shillings (30p). Service was provided on board by 'an alert domestic and a courteous conductor'. ('Note sur les voitures a dormir de divers systèmes en essai sur les chemins de fer anglais' D. Banderali, August 1874.)

According to the author of the above remark the Pullman trains aroused considerable controversy between those who were in favour and those who said that the advantages of comfort and likely attraction of traffic from other lines in competition with the Midland did not outweigh the extra cost involved in hauling these heavier trains. He also pointed out that if ordinary Midland stock had been used for the ordinary passenger the total train weight would have been less. Banderali in his notes compared the Midlands' Pullman sleeper with the North British Company's car of 1873, the first to run on a British railway for ordinary passengers, and Richard Blore's sleeping car built for the London & North Western Railway in 1874.

At the Midlands' St Pancras terminus in London the erection of a special ticket office for Pullman passengers only was approved by the Traffic Committee on 15 December 1874.

It is worth here describing the Midland day cars used in the Pullman train, which as previously noted were of two types. The first/second class composite car had accommodation for 32 second class passengers accommodated in four compartments at one end of the car with access from a side corridor which changed sides at the centre of the vehicle to serve a further three compartments each seating six first class passengers (three per side). From the other side, there was a door dividing off first and second class areas in the cross corridor and at each end of the car beyond the compartments was a vestibule and a lavatory compartment. Upholstery and fittings were Midland standard with, as before mentioned, blue cloth for the first class compartments and green for the second class, and in that respect were the same as ordinary Midland stock of the period, but of course the side corridors were a completely new innovation on Midland trains and were hardly to be found elsewhere in Britain.

The other type of Midland day car of Pullman external appearance was the third class baggage brake which had an open saloon with transverse seats trimmed in red cloth, and seating 32 passengers. Beyond this saloon was a smoking compartment with 18 loose detachable armchairs, 'which could easily take more passengers at times of peak loading'. Overall length was given as 18.5m and overall width 2.9m. These day cars proved not to be popular with the travelling public who regarded them as distinctly un-English and Banderali reports that the parlour cars were regarded by him as absolutely useless, but that the sleeping cars proved popular, although that is going slightly ahead of our story.

The Carriage & Wagon Committee heard an explanation on 30 June 1874 as to the desirability of altering the couplings on the Pullman cars so as they would couple with the Midlands' ordinary stock, since as built the early cars had the Miller centre coupler. This matter was reported to the General Purposes Committee for approval.

By this time the Pullman Company had established itself in both London and Paris with offices at 76-77 Cheapside, London, under the English manager John Miller and at 1 Rue de Quatre Septembre, and near to the Paris stock exchange, under Colonel Georges Guorand.

On 6 June 1874 the prototype sleeping car 'Midland' was withdrawn from service on the Midland Railway and sent across the Channel with Guorand, Manager of the Paris office, who travelled in the vehicle all the way to Italy via the Mont Cenis pass as the first stage of an extensive tour to sell Pullmans in Europe.

After signing a contract with the Upper Italian Railway and the Mediolanum Railway for their Indian Mail train to Brindisi, a trial contract was also signed with the Roman Railway Company for a Florence-Rome-Naples service.

Guorand then travelled in 'Midland' over the Semmering Pass to Vienna where he began negotiations for a Pullman service between Berlin and Rome. He was not successful, despite enthusiasm for the project by the South Austrian Railways who were owners of a large part of the route.

The sleeping car 'Midland' did not return to the Midland Railway until 20 June 1877 when it went immediately into the Derby Pullman car shops to be rebuilt to the standard pattern of sleeper, which had by this time been established and which involved changing the sofa sections running along the vehicle sides beneath the windows into the standard cross-section which comprised a pair of facing seats below each upper berth having a table between them during the day. For night-time use the table was stored below and the two seat squabs pulled towards each other until touching which, together with the seat back which dropped down, formed a comfortable lower berth.

The story of 'Midland' and the return to Derby is recounted later.

3 Pullman Services

Returning now to activities at Derby — the Midland Company set their rivals by the ears by announcing that as from 1 January 1875 it was abolishing entirely second class travel. The railway world became excited at the announcement and of course the Midland's competitors were up in arms at the proposal.

In line with this decision Allport wrote on 19 January 1875 to request that the second class compartments in the Pullman cars be altered and trimmed with blue cloth and made first class, and also that all the smoking compartments in the composite first/second day cars be done away with and provision for first class smokers be made in one end of the third class cars which was to be trimmed and fitted up as first class.

A plan for providing additional shed accommodation for the Pullman cars at Derby was put before the Traffic Committee on 16 February 1875 and referred to the Carriage & Wagon Committee. This matter passed through various committees and the cost of such accommodation was reported as £1,624 13s 5d (£1,624.67). The Midland Board duly approved of the work on 5 May 1875, the Pullman Car Company being required to pay rent for the same and the site as should be fixed by the General Manager and the Carriage & Wagon Superintendent, Mr Thomas Gething Clayton, who was asked to report on the matter to the C&W Committee on 6 July 1875 and in the meantime prepare a plan and an estimate of the cost for the General Purposes Committee.

In the meantime George Pullman had presented his final bill for a balance of £5,392 19s 8d (£5,392.98) for the Midland day cars, the cost of which was: third class, £1,182 11s 2d (£1,182.56) each and composites £1,968 19s 6d (£1,968.97½) each. The Midland Board drew a cheque for £4,000 as an initial payment against the final bill, the total of which amounted to £7,875 17s 1d (£7,875.85½) for the composites and £4,730 4s 10d (£4,730.24) for the third class baggage cars, and then referred the matter to the Carriage & Wagon Committee for approval. Clayton duly reported to them that while he had examined the account he had no means whatever of checking either the quantities or prices of the materials, or of the labour expended in their construction and therefore recommended that the account be passed for payment in good faith with the Pullman Palace Car Company.

After considering returns from the initial Pullman service from Bradford to London a new service was initiated on 1 April 1875 between London (St Pancras) and Liverpool consisting of day trains with a sleeping car service to Liverpool from St Pancras leaving at midnight. These trains utilised the newly opened Marple curve, built to connect the Midland and Cheshire Lines' systems.

After careful watch on the returns of passengers using the various services, it was resolved to try to speed up the 9.20am Pullman service from Bradford and this was duly done, deleting the stops at Chesterfield and Trent and arriving in St Pancras at 2.15pm. From 2 August 1875, a year later, the Trent stop was re-introduced and arrival at St Pancras became 2.20pm. This arrangement was kept until the opening of the Settle-Carlise line for passenger traffic, the goods traffic opening coinciding with this last alteration to the 'Bradford Pullman'.

During 1874 three sleeping cars, three parlour cars and eight non-supplement day cars had been completed at Derby, and by the time the Liverpool service began, more crates of parts for further sleeping and parlour cars had arrived for assembly.

Among the first of the new cars constructed at Derby in 1875 were the parlour car 'Ohio' and the sleeping car 'Ocean' fitted up for day use, which went off to the Great Northern Railway from Derby and were placed in trial service by that company between London (King's Cross) and Manchester (London Road) stations. They worked the 'Manchester Saloon' service jointly with the Manchester, Sheffield and Lincolnshire Railway via Sheffield, leaving King's Cross at 10.10am and Manchester at 10am respectively, both return journeys commencing at 5pm.

Also completed during 1875 were a further three sleeping cars ('St George', 'Princess' and 'Transit') and two parlour cars ('Jupiter' and 'Saturn') for the Midland and the sleeping car 'Mars' which went directly to the London, Brighton & South Coast Railway on 26 October 1875. 'Mars' had its seating arranged permanently for day use and worked the very first London-Brighton Pullman service.

On 6 October 1875 the Board heard from Mr Allport the proposed clauses of the supplemental Pullman agreement to which he had received the assent of the Pullman Palace Car Company, together with a 'slight verbal alteration to make its meaning more clear' and that Mr A. B. Pullman would bring the sealed copy with him on his next visit to England, which Mr Allport expected would be during that month.

The Midland Board, at their 5 April 1876 meeting, requested the General Manager to furnish a statement showing the number of cars running on the railway, the number of cars for which requisitions had been furnished, where the cars were running and the receipts which the Midland Company had earned by them.

On 7 June Mr Allport stated that requisitions had already been issued for 24 drawing-room cars and 12 sleeping cars, and he gave the statistics requested. After hearing the report, it was resolved 'that the sanction of the Board be obtained before any further requisitions are made for Pullman cars, and that Mr Allport prepare a statement for the last half-year and the current half-year showing earnings to the Midland Company per Pullman carriage per mile run'. The supplementary agreement with the Pullman Car Company was postponed for future consideration.

Allport duly reported on 2 August, when the Board resolved that the matter be referred to the accountant to 'compile a statement showing the earnings of Pullman cars per car/mile for each of the trains in which they are run, separating sleeping cars from parlour cars, and making comparison with like information as to Midland carriages', and also 'that he obtain and submit such other information as may bear the cost of running the Pullman cars'.

On 1 May 1876 the Midland's own new direct route to Scotland via their costly Settle-Carlisle line was at last opened for passenger traffic and with it came a new Pullman sleeper and parlour car service to Glasgow (St Enoch's) via the Glasgow and South Western Railway.

Prior to the event the *Carlisle Journal* of 2 May 1876 records that a special inspection train with Midland directors aboard the brand new parlour car 'Venus' carried out a detailed tour of the line which took two days — Tuesday and Wednesday, 25 and 26 April. The *Sheffield and Rotherham Independent* newspaper reported that those aboard included Edward Shipley Ellis, Sir Isaac Morley, James Allport, Carter, Thompson, the vice chairman, Messrs Mappin and Thomas (directors), J. S. Crossley, Engineer of the line, with his successor Johnston and I. H. Sanders, the Midland Company's architect who had been responsible for the design of the stations and other buildings along the line.

The paper reported that the company scorned the comfort of 'Venus' and travelled in an open cattle truck, fitted with wooden benches, in order to see the line better!

Advertisements for the new line appeared in the local press and of course the new services were detailed in the timetables. One general advertisement for the line read as follows:

Midland Railway
New Route between England and Scotland

'The Settle & Carlisle Railway is now open for Passenger Traffic, and an entirely New Service of Express and Fast Trains has been established between the Midland System and Scotland.

'A Morning Express Train runs between London and Edinburgh and Glasgow, in each direction, with Pullman Drawing-Room Cars attached, and a Night Express Train runs in each direction between the same places, with Pullman Sleeping Cars attached. First-Class Passengers may avail themselves of the comfort and convenience of these luxurious Cars on payment of a small charge in addition to the Railway Fare, particulars of which may be ascertained at the Stations.

'For the convenience of Passengers to and from the West of England and Scotland, a New Service of Express Passenger Trains has been established to and from Bristol, Bath, Gloucester, and Birmingham, in connection with the Through Service between London and Edinburgh and Glasgow. The Up and Down Day Express Trains stop half-an-hour at Normanton, in all cases, to enable Passengers to dine. A spacious and comfortable Dining Room is provided at that Station for their accommodation.

'Through Guards, in charge of the Luggage of Passengers, travel between London and Edinburgh and Glasgow by the Day and Night Express Trains in both directions.

'Passengers by this Route by the Express Trains between London and Edinburgh and Glasgow are conveyed in Through Carriages of the most improved description, fitted with the Westinghouse Continuous Brake and all the most approved modern appliances.

'Ordinary Return tickets between Stations in England and Stations in Scotland are available for the Return Journey on any day within One Calendar Month of the date of issue.

Derby, 1877   *JAMES ALLPORT*, General Manager'

After the opening the new Pullman service began in earnest. A Pullman express left St Pancras at 9.15pm reaching Derby at 11.55pm and departing from Leeds at 2.08am connecting at Shipley with the 2.15am from Bradford. On reaching Skipton at 2.49am the train split the Edinburgh portion leaving at 2.55am and running non-stop to Carlisle, which it reached at 4.55am. It eventually arrived in Edinburgh, having travelled over the North British Railway, at 7.35am making connections for Perth (arr 10.00am), Dundee (arr 11.20am), Aberdeen (arr 4.05pm) and Inverness (arr 6.25pm). Motive power over the Midland was Kirtley's '890' class 2-4-0s (soon replaced), whilst the North British had a new type of 4-4-0 express locomotive with 6ft 6in wheels, designed by Dugald Drummond and built by Neilson & Co of Glasgow and the North British itself.

The Glasgow portion of the 'Pullman' sleeper left Skipton at 3.05am also running non-stop to Carlisle (arr 5.05am) and then to Glasgow (St Enoch) (arr 8.00am).

For motive power the Glasgow & South Western Railway used its 7ft 1in driving wheeled 4-4-0s designed by James Stirling, which were equipped with Westinghouse air brake equipment.

The day time drawing-room car express left St Pancras at 10.30am calling at Derby (1.00pm), Leeds (3.10pm), Shipley (for connection with the 3.15pm from Bradford) leaving at 3.30pm, Bingley (3.38pm), Keighley (3.45pm) and Skipton (4.02pm), where it made a connection for passengers from Liverpool and Manchester via the Colne line (having left at 2.00pm and 2.20pm respectively) and where the train split. The Edinburgh portion, with its drawing-room car, left at 4.18pm arriving at Carlisle at 6.18pm and Edinburgh (via the NBR) at 9.15pm with connections to Perth (11.35pm), Dundee (12.50am), Aberdeen (3.20am), and Inverness (8.55am). The Glasgow 'Pullman' left Skipton at 4.30pm arriving at Carlisle at 6.30pm and Glasgow (St Enoch), via the G&SWR, at 9.20pm.

In the reverse direction the first 'up' Pullman sleeper left Carlisle for London at 12.08am, its connecting times for those travelling from further north being Inverness 10.18am, Aberdeen 12.23pm, Dundee 3.03pm, Perth 4.20pm and Edinburgh 9.20pm, and arrived at Skipton at 2.08am, where it was joined by the Glasgow 'up' sleeper which had departed at 9.15pm and left Carlisle at 12.18am. Both parts joined the sleeper continued southwards from Skipton at 2.25am reaching Shipley at 2.47am to await the arrival of the Bradford connection at 3.00am. The train then reached Leeds at 3.10am and St Pancras at 8am.

The 'up' Pullman day-time drawing-room car trains ran as follows:

Glasgow (depart 10.15am) and Carlisle (depart 1.05pm) arriving at Skipton at 3.05pm where it was joined by the Edinburgh portion which had left at 10.25am with passengers from Inverness (7.35pm) and Perth (6am) leaving Carlisle at 1.15pm and arriving at Skipton 3.15pm. Here both portions were joined, leaving at 3.28pm, calling at Keighley at 3.42pm, Shipley (to set down for Bradford only, arriving at 4.10pm), Leeds 4.10pm and London (St Pancras) at 9.05pm.

On Sundays only one train — the 'Pullman' sleeping car express — ran in each direction. The 'down' train left St Pancras at 9.15pm Saturday evening and ran complete as far as Carlisle, where it arrived at 4.55am, and where it was split for Edinburgh (7.35am), Glasgow (8am), Dundee (11.20am), Perth (10am), Aberdeen (4.05pm) and Inverness (6.25pm).

The 'up' train left Carlisle at 12.18am with passengers from Inverness (10.18am Saturday morning), Aberdeen (12.23pm), Perth (4.20pm), Dundee (3.03pm), Glasgow (9.15pm) and Edinburgh (9.20pm). The train reached Skipton at 2.18am and left at 2.25am, stopping at Shipley (for Bradford, arr 3.00am), Leeds (3.10am) and St Pancras 8.00am.

As a result of this new service the complete Pullman trains of the original service

26

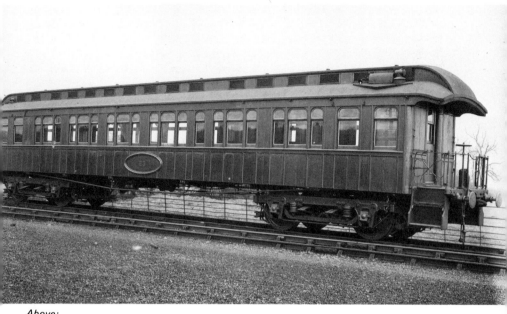

Above:
Pullman sleeping car No 23, built originally as 'Princess' in July 1875, and renumbered 23 in 1888 following purchase of all of the sleeping cars from the Pullman Company. *Author's Collection*

Below:
Pullman drawing room car No 8, built as 'Albion' and put into traffic on 9 October 1876. The photograph clearly shows the ornate decorative lining out with which the car was embellished. *British Railways, LMR*

27

between Bradford and London were discontinued on 14-15 May 1876 and Midland carriages substituted on similarly timed service trains. It must be admitted that the day cars and parlour cars had not been over-popular with the travelling public, and earnings from travelling in the latter were on the low side. The General Manager reported on the matter and on 31 October 1876 the Carriage & Wagon Committee considered plans showing how the cars could be altered so as to be 'more conveniently adapted for the traffic'. Six Midland Pullman cars were altered at a cost of £1,340 which was charged to revenue.

Further alterations requested involved the fitting of eight parlour cars and six sleeping cars with Westinghouse automatic brake equipment at a cost of £369 7s 4d (£369.37), but on 6 February 1877 the General Purposes Committee refused approval. In addition the Board, whilst agreeing to pay a bill for £161 11s 8d (£161.59) for sundry repairs done by the Pullman Company to cars in service, declared that in future no work was to be done by them for the Midland without a requisition from the Carriage & Wagon Superintendent, T. G. Clayton. Clearly things were not going too well!

On 13 November 1876 the Pullman car fares on trains were reduced in a bid to encourage wider use of the facilities.

During 1876 parlour cars 'Mercury', 'Juno', 'Venus', 'Vesta', 'Minerva', 'Planet', 'Albion', 'Comet', and 'Ariel', had been completed and sleeping cars 'Saxon', 'Castalia', 'Scotia', 'Norman', 'Australia', 'India' and 'Germania' were outshopped. These were followed in 1877 by parlour cars 'Aurora', 'Ceres', 'Eclipse' and 'Alexandra' which completed building for the time being for the Midland.

Three further parlour cars were completed later in 1877, these being 'Alexandra' (II) and 'Albert Edward', which both went direct to the London, Brighton & South Coast line on 10 October 1877 and 'Globe' which was kept in reserve at Derby as a spare car following completion in November 1877.

It was reported to the Traffic Committee (Min 20567) on 2 January 1877 that the London & North Western Railway Company had reduced the charge for sleeping car berths on their services between London (Euston) and Glasgow (Central) and Edinburgh (Princes Street), and it was resolved 'that this informtion be communicated to the Pullman Car Company with a view to their considering how far it will affect the traffic carried in their sleeping cars'.

From 1 February 1877 a new service with Pullman cars was introduced between Leeds, Birmingham and Bristol.

On 1 May 1877 Allport reported to the Board that he had received communication from General Porter, Vice President of the Pullman Palace Car Company proposing that they undertake the maintenance of the Pullman cars for the unexpired term of the agreement at cost price.

After some discussion it was resolved that the Midland Company prefer to adhere to the provisions of the agreement and retain the maintenance in their own hands. Clearly this did not include the interiors for on 16 October 1877 the Carriage & Wagon Committee considered a request from the Pullman Car Company that the Midland Company undertake the maintenance of the upholstery in the cars at the Pullman Company's expense and Mr Clayton was requested to obtain proper terms in writing and report further.

By 11 November the Pullman Company had completed the construction of all the cars then on order and dispensed with their workforce, withdrawing their foreman and manager back to America, and applied to the Midland Company for them to purchase a quantity of spare material and fittings suitable for repairs and maintenance of the cars working on the Midland. The price had been a greatly reduced one and had been agreed between the Pullman Company and Mr Clayton and it was resolved that the materials in question be purchased for £836 14s 6d (£836.72½). Further, through the Pullman shops being closed, the Midland Company undertook to carry out repairs to upholstery in the cars, charging them for any work done.

A list of all the Pullman cars then in service with the dates into traffic was given as below:

Parlour cars	Into traffic	Sleeping cars	Into traffic
'Victoria'	June 1874	'Excelsior'	June 1874
'Britannia'	June 1874	'Enterprise'	June 1874
'Leo'	June 1874	'St George'	28 June 1875
'Jupiter'	23 August 1874	'Princess'	17 July 1875
'Saturn'	10 September 1875	'Transit'	13 October 1875
'Mercury'	28 April 1876	'Saxon'	4 February 1876
'Juno'	28 April 1876	'Castalia'	28 April 1876
'Venus'	3 May 1876	'Scotia'	28 April 1876
'Vesta'	28 July 1876	'Norman'	2 June 1876
'Minerva'	28 July 1876	'Australia'	20 June 1876
'Planet'	27 September 1876	'India'	28 July 1876
'Albion'	9 October 1876	'Germania'	26 August 1876
'Comet'	31 October 1876	'Midland'	June 1877
'Ariel'	31 October 1876		
'Apollo'	19 January 1877		
'Adonis'	19 January 1877		
'Aurora'	1 May 1877		
'Ceres'	1 May 1877		
'Eclipse'	10 July 1877		
'Alexandra'(I)	10 July 1877		
'Globe'	Still in shops, not been in traffic		

Notes:
'Midland' went on the Continent July 1874. Returned 20 June 1877.
'Mars' went to Brighton 26 October 1875.
'Alexandra' (II) went to Brighton 10 October 1877.
'Albert Edward' went to Brighton 10 October 1877.

C&W minute 773 of 6 November 1877.

Regarding the sleeping car 'Midland, which as previously recorded went on a sales mission to the Continent, C&W minute 776 of 20 November 1877 is worthy of repeating:

'This car which has been over on the continent for about three years was brought back to England in June last, and the first I heard respecting it was from my London foreman, the Pullman people having applied to him to render them assistance in getting the car on the rails at the docks at Poplar. He asked my permission which was given, but in the interval the car was got on by someone else and brought round by the North London Railway to St Pancras station. Upon the application of the Pullman Car Company we made the car that it would couple up with our trains that it might come to their shops at Derby and we charged them with the cost. The Pullman Car Company then put the car into good order, altered the drawgear and buffers to our standard in their own shops, after which the car was sent to work in the Scotch traffic. The first trace we have of its working was on 30 August last, it has been on these trains since that date.'

It is worth recording as a footnote at this point that there is evidence to suggest that the Pullman cars delivered to the Midland Railway at Derby in kit form were not all new, and that some had in fact already been in service in America before being dismantled, refurbished and then packed up for shipment to England.

Below:
Pullman drawing room or parlour car No 13, formerly 'Eclipse' at Derby. Completed on 10 July 1877, the car had become a third class saloon by 1890.
R. J. Essery collection courtesy HMRS

4 Competition and Catering

In 1878 the first meal both cooked and served on a British train was eaten in a Pullman car which was part of a train of vehicles specially hired by a private party which travelled all the way from London to Wick and back. The train comprised a Pullman sleeping car, a Pullman parlour car and two Midland vans fitted out for the purpose, one as a kitchen and the other to serve as a bathroom complete with bath. The special train ran over the Midland via the Settle & Carlisle line and thence via the Glasgow and South Western and Highland Railways.

Early in January 1878 the Traffic Committee had carefully considered the monthly returns, and decided to take two of the Pullman cars earning the least revenue per mile out of service. By 5 June the earnings having duly been reported to the Board, the latter resolved that the low level of these be drawn to the attention of the Traffic Committee with a request that they report to the Board what cars they think ought to be withdrawn.

On 11 March 1878 the complete trains of Pullman cars with non-supplement day cars, was re-introduced, this time between London (St Pancras), Liverpool and Manchester. These trains were fitted with Smith's vacuum brake throughout and the first and third class day cars had been improved since being withdrawn in May 1876 and had also been repainted.

The service comprised a train at 5pm from London serving Liverpool and Manchester and a service in the opposite direction leaving Liverpool at 10.45am and Manchester at 11.25am. However, after only eight days it became obvious that the public still disliked the day cars and the service was discontinued on Tuesday 19 March being replaced by ordinary Midland carriages plus a drawing-room car. Thereafter the day cars were only in occasional use for special parties until 1884.

A record of the running of the London to Manchester service from Leicester onwards and conveying a Pullman parlour car and nine ordinary carriages hauled by Johnson 4-4-0 No 1292 as far as Derby and No 1293 beyond was made by C. E. Stretton and is included in Appendix 8 along with the leg of a run from St Pancras to Leicester behind 4-4-0 No 1328.

At their meeting on 2 July 1878 the Traffic Committee considered the returns for their new Pullman services from Leeds to Birmingham and Bristol and resolved that since receipts were low this service should be discontinued.

This recommendation was considered by the Board on 3 July and it was resolved that the existing arrangement between the Company and the Pullman Car Company for greasing the Pullman cars in the Scotch trains be extended (to expire at the same time) to the Pullman cars running in the London and Liverpool and Manchester trains.

Mr Allport stated that Mr George Pullman would be in England in a few days whereupon the Board considered it desirable that Mr Pullman should be seen for the purpose of discussing the modifications in the agreement with him which may be necessary and also of discussing with him that he should become the Agent for the Midland Company in America.

It was resolved that the deputy Chairman, Mr Kenrick and Mr Jones with Mr Allport and Mr Beale (solicitor) be approached to meet Mr Pullman and discuss these subjects with him, reporting on the same at the midmonth Board.

The Pullman services between Leeds, Birmingham and Bristol were terminated on 1 October 1878 and the drawing-room cars were withdrawn, and in addition the Perth night expresses, as Stretton calls them, were withdrawn for the winter period as they had been the previous year. These Perth trains had been re-introduced on 1 July 1878 (following withdrawal on 1 October 1877 for the winter months), with a Pullman sleeper attached, but some competition was introduced by the Great Northern Railway who, on 19 August of that year, began their own opposition service between London and Perth.

One further change in services was the withdrawal of the Pullman drawing-room cars running between London and Leeds, which were taken off and run to and from Liverpool instead as from the first week of August 1878.

On 20 August the Traffic Committee considered a letter from Mr Clements, solicitor for the Pullman Car Company, approving a memorandum of a meeting held between the Midland and George Pullman on 23 July 1878, and stated that 'it is within the competence of the Midland Company under the original agreement to discontinue carriages which are not remunerative; that the valuation of the dilapidation upon the carriages given up can be made without any new agreement, and that the other paragraphs of the Memorandum can form an independent agreement between the Midland and Pullman Companies without varying the original agreement'. The matter was referred to the Board.

The following month, the 20th to be exact, the need for converting the sheds at Derby formerly used by the Pullman Company so as to be again available for the purpose of repairing the Pullman cars in accordance with the arrangements made with that Company was considered and it was resolved that it be referred to the Midland Board.

On 8 August 1878 the Pullman Car Company and the Midland Company signed a new agreement. This provided for the Pullman Company to appoint and pay the salary of a manager to run the shops at Derby and Mr Augustus Rapp was duly appointed to that position with the approval of the Midland Company. It was agreed that any successor should also require the approval of the Company. All men working in the Pullman shops should be employed or dismissed by this manager. The full minute reads:

'Gentlemen,

'For your information, I beg to say that it has been arranged for Mr Rapp to take charge of the maintenance of the Pullman cars on 1 October next. He will have an assistant to keep his accounts and overlook the shop in his absence and to take charge of the stores and materials and timekeeping, the Assistant's wages to be £3 10s (£3.50) per week. He will also have a foreman to take charge of repairs, painting etc, of the cars at Derby at £2 15s (£2.75) per week, also an out-door man to take charge of the running of the cars and the lifting of them at out-stations at £2 15s (£2.75) per week, besides this there will be the requisite number of workmen at ordinary wages.

'Mr Rapp taking charge of the lubrication of the cars, intended to place two additional men at St Pancras, two at Leicester, one at Derby, one at Liverpool and Manchester, two at Normanton and one at Carlisle to lubricate the axle boxes instead of having men travelling with the cars.

'This will involve a special staff for superintending the Pullman cars with salaries amounting to £1,016 16s (£1,016.80) per annum, exclusive of Mr Rapp's salary.

'All materials Mr Rapp may require he will get from my department by requisition. The time taking of his men will be performed precisely in the same way as other men and a separate pay bill will be made out weekly and one of our present Pay Clerks will pay the wages every week.

'I am gentlemen, Your obedient service, Thos G. Clayton.'

To assist Rapp, Messrs Longstreet and Wildlagen were appointed to look after the operating side and Mr Joseph Monck was appointed to oversee technical matters.

Rapp has been described as a 'big, impressive German-American' who was the chief designer at 'Pullman City'. According to Pratt it was George Pullman's decision that the technical man who had drawn up the plans should be responsible and assign to each section of the car its proper location during assembly and therefore Rapp's appointment at Derby was in line with this general policy.

The Pullman staff made many friends at Derby, particularly among the Freemasons, and were to stay in the town for the remaining period of the Pullman contract, Rapp taking up residence in a house in Barlow Street.

Wildlagen is believed to have been Rapp's nephew, but little is known of him or Mr Longstreet.

Mr Joseph Monck, an Irish-American has been described as 'one of the best, cosmopolitan, affable and somewhat devout'.

The two sheds at Derby, formerly occupied by the Pullman Company were set aside as a repair depot for all the cars in service and all materials, wages, clerkage was to be paid for by the Midland Company. Rapp would forward requests for materials to the Company and would provide a monthly statement to the Carriage & Wagon Committee on the costs of maintenance and a quarterly statement on the conditon of all the cars.

The Midland Company would pay Rapp's salary, and also afford facilities for the erection of cars for other Companies on reasonable terms provided that such work did not interfere with the use of the shops for servicing Midland Pullman cars.

This agreement was to run for three years and henceforward until six months notice be given by either party.

5 Problems in Service

On 2 April 1878 the Carriage & Wagon Committee considered the overheating of axle boxes which was put down to bad construction and poor lubrication, together with the great weight of the cars resting upon them. The minute is reproduced here in full:

'I have to report that ever since the Pullman cars commenced running upon the railway we have had great difficulty with the journals running hot.

'Everything has been done that could be to make them run cool from the very first, both by the Pullman people themselves and also by us.

'All through the time they have been in traffic, oils of the very best description have been obtained and used without the desired effect. Mixtures of oil, sulphur, black lead, and plumbago, all of which have a tendency to keep the journals cool, phospho-bronze and other special kinds of bearings have been tried and every possible care has been taken. Men have travelled with the cars for weeks together to pay special attention to them, and at our various terminal stations the Pullman cars have received more attention and given us more trouble than all the other stock. At intermediate stations the cars have had special attention and taken up the examiners' time which has on very many occasions been to the detriment and neglect of the other vehicles on the train.

'I attribute their running hot to two causes:

'First: The bad construction of the axleboxes and mode of lubrication.

'Second: To the great weight there is upon the journals. The number of hot journals in proportion to the number of cars in traffic is the same now as when the first few cars began to run, and I really see no way to cure it without going to the expense of making a different class of axle box, but this is a difficult matter because it involves other alterations in the bogie frame and axleguards and the cost of which is estimated at £27 10s (£27.50) per car.'

The matter was referred to the General Purposes Committee for approval.

Other operating problems included the bursting or uncoupling of brake hoses, breaking of drawhooks and screw couplings, and brakes sticking in the 'on' position. Pullman cars were mostly fitted with the Westinghouse automatic air brake, but parlour cars 'Albion', 'Comet', 'Alexandra' and 'Britannia' were fitted with Sanders and Bolitho's automatic brake as was the sleeping car 'St George', all during 1880. These were used to work the services to Liverpool and Manchester.

On 3 September 1878 the C&W Committee received an application from the Pullman Company to borrow two trucks (bogies) until after the end of September, to help them out of a temporary shortage, the original approach to buy these outright

carriage roof lamps at a cost to revenue of £139.

By 17 December 1878 the Carriage & Wagon Committee were discussing Pullmans again when the difficulties of coupling them up to ordinary stock was raised, some having become uncoupled during journeys, relying entirely on the side chains. It was agreed that six cars be fitted up with buffers and ordinary draw gear as an experiment.

Some idea of the costs of operating the Pullman cars on the Midland can be gained from the fact that Mr Jones reported to the same committee that maintenance costs for the months of November and December 1878 and January and February 1879 had amounted to £1,693 5s 8d (£1,693.28).

On 26 April 1879 the much travelled prototype sleeping car 'Midland' was off on its travels again, this time demonstrating the benefits of the Pullman car to the Directors of the Great Northern Railway who ran it on the East Coast route some 33,592 miles before returning it on 10 July of the same year. The Midland accountant considered 'Midland' to be equal to two ordinary first class carriages, and therefore 'the GNR should pay twice the rate for the mileage covered, amounting to £209 19s (£209.95) or $1\frac{1}{2}$d (1p) per mile'.

On 1 July 1879 the new Midland Scottish Joint Stock vehicles began running in the 'Scotch' express trains and Pullman cars fitted with normal buffers were included in the train formations. From 31 July the Perth night expresses were re-introduced for the summer, composed of new MSJS stock and a Pullman sleeper, and ran as usual until 1 October. These trains were the 8pm from London to Perth and the 7.35pm in the reverse direction.

In the autumn of 1879 the North British Railway were in touch concerning Pullmans as follows:

'Kippenross, Dunblane,
18 September 1879

Sir,

We have been looking into expenses and one point we all agree upon is too many carriages are run in the trains. It increases the cost of fuel, the wear and tear of the road, and particularly our carriage repairs. Our through passengers are very few in winter and I am asked to write to see if the Midland would drop the day Pullman from Edinboro' to Carlisle on 1 October for the winter months. We are carrying very few passengers in it and I do not believe we shall have two a day, even now we have not much more. I would not propose this if the East Coast run a day one, but theirs is only at night.

Please let me hear from you soon.

Yours truly
J. Stirling'

It was agreed by the Board at their meeting on 1 October that the Pullman parlour cars be withdrawn on the day service in which they had been running since the opening of the line to Edinburgh, and from this date private parties were allowed to engage a Pullman car for journeys of over 100 miles on payment of a sum equal to 10 first class fares plus the Pullman supplement.

The date 1 November 1879 is a significant one, for it was on that day that the first regular dining car service began on a British railway. The railway company was not, however, the Midland but the Great Northern and the service was between London (King's Cross) and Leeds using the dining car 'Prince of Wales'. This vehicle had been completed at Derby as a standard parlour car in 1875 and named 'Ohio' and had gone directly to the GNR in company with standard sleeping car 'Ocean' fitted up for day use. The pair worked in a service over the Great Northern and the Manchester, Sheffield & Lincolnshire Railways between London (King's Cross) and Manchester (London Road) via Sheffield.

'Ohio' was returned to the Pullman shops at Derby in 1878 where the car was rebuilt as a dining car and renamed 'Prince of Wales'. It returned to the GNR where it made a special demonstration run from King's Cross to Peterborough and back prior to the introduction of the new service.

Its introduction only came about however, following a long series of negotiations. By 26 October 1877 the directors of the Great Northern Railway Company were being urged by George Pullman to accept sleeping cars for service in their East Coast trains between London and Edinburgh. They instructed Henry Oakley, the General Manager to write to Pullman to ascertain 'whether he could propose any modified form of carriage which would be less unsightly and cumbersome than the one proposed'.

The next firm proposals are contained in a letter from H. S. Roberts, Manager of the Pullman Palace Car Company (Europe) in which he stated:

'I enclose herewith a drawing of the interior of one of our cars showing the modifications and changes which we propose to make in the car to suit your services. We propose to make the drawing room and the smoking room into one large refreshment room shut off by a door, which I have marked "A" on the plan, from the main part of the car. The seats in this smoking room would be raised high enough so that the head can rest against them, and would also have movable arms between each seat at this end of the car. We have also provided a closet for bottles and glasses, etc.

'I would propose to alter in our own shops, ie at Derby, three of our cars for your service, one to be used as a spare, and I shall be much obliged if you will bring the matter before your Board at the next meeting, so that if it is decided to have three cars we can proceed with the work as early as possible.

'I believe if a car of this kind was run through on your ten o'clock express to Glasgow it would pay very well.'

Oakley duly submitted the proposals to the board of the GNR stating:

'I submit herewith a proposal from the Pullman Palace Company to supply us with a day car for our ten o'clock 'Scotch Express' which they will fit up, if we like, with accommodation for refreshments so that travellers can obtain foods, etc on the journey after the fashion of the dining-room saloons on the American Railways.

'They will undertake at their own expense to let us have the car to run as an experiment without any obligation for a term, undertaking to finance it at any time on reasonable notice and conducting themselves with such receipts as they can collect from passengers on the journey.

'The only damage the Company would suffer would therefore be the haulage of the car if it was unsuccessful, but as this can be terminated at three months notice, the risk

Above:
The interior of the Pullman dining saloon in the Great Northern Railway's 'Prince of Wales'. *Illustrated London News*

Below:
The interior of the smoking saloon and the kitchen verandah showing the cook's assistant (his son) hard at work. *Illustrated London News*

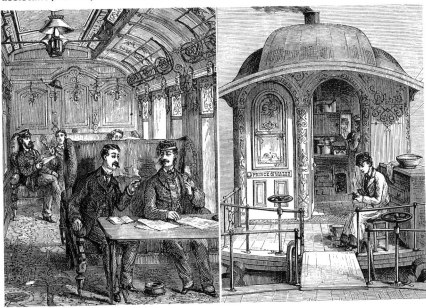

in that respect would not be serious. I have told the PCC that I would ask for your instructions.'

It was decided to go ahead with such a vehicle and on 22 October 1879 Oakley wrote to the directors stating that the car was now ready and that it was proposed to put it into the 10am train from Leeds to London returning to Leeds by the 5.30pm train, commencing on 1 November. He went on:

'The car has been fitted with a large general saloon capable of seating 11 persons with revolving chairs and with means of affixing a table between each two after the practice adopted (I am told) in America. A second smaller saloon is also provided which will hold nine, included for those who desire to smoke.

'The kitchen apparatus has been partitioned off and is furnished with a stove capable of cooking all sorts of food for 20 persons.

'By way of experiment it was run down to Peterborough and back on Saturday (note — this was Saturday 18 October 1879) when we invited several representatives of the London press to inspect it. A very good dinner was cooked in the car and served much to the satisfaction of all. Mr Tennant, MP, our Director accompanied the trip down, but left us at Peterboro' where Sir Andrew Fairbairn, who was accidentally coming up, joined us on the return journey.

'It has been agreed that the car should be sent to Leeds and representatives of the local press of Leeds and Bradford and a few of our chief supporters should be invited to take a trip in it, and I shall be glad if the Directors will give instruction on this point.

'The car weighs 22 tons and will of course be a serious addition to the weight of the train. At this season of the year, however, we think that by reducing the number of carriages now run on it by three we shall be able to keep time.'

In charge of the car for that day was the Pullman Car Company's own conductor James Bower, who had come over from Chicago where he had served as conductor on the first dining car to run between Chicago and Buffalo late in 1875, and who subsequently made his name in England. James had run away to sea at the age of 14 from his home in Portsmouth, settling later in Chicago. He returned to England in 1877 with Pullman and worked on the Midland Railway Pullman services before his GNR debut.

The new service was reported in *The Illustrated London News* for 22 November 1879.

'The Pullman Dining Car

'The Great Northern Railway Company has been the first in England to adopt this comfortable American system, which has been daily in operation, since 1 November, in one train each way between Leeds and London. The Pullman Palace Car Company, whose sleeping and drawing-room cars are in use upon several English and Scottish railways, have provided for the Great Northern line a handsome and convenient new carriage, the chief interior apartments of which are shown in our illustrations. It was constructed at Detroit, in the United States, at a cost of £3,000. It is 52ft in length, 8ft in breadth, and runs upon eight wheels. It comprises a dining-saloon, in the middle, a kitchen behind, and a smoking-room in front, with steward's pantry, ladies' dressing

40

room, gentlemen's lavatory, cupboards, and stoves. The dining-saloon has six tables, three on each side, as represented in our illustration; there are 10 easy chairs, large, well-stuffed, and covered with crimson velvet, each revolving on a solid pivot. The ladies' dressing-room, which adjoins this, has a stove, enclosed in a metal-lined wooden cupboard. The sides or walls of the saloon are of American black walnut, decorated with veneer of French walnut. The smoking-room, of which we also give an illustration, has two tables, and seats for nine persons. There are electric bells to summon the attendants, who are the cook, the steward or waiter, and the boy of the smoking-room. The refreshments, including wines, are supplied by Pullman's Company at ordinary hotel dinner charges. Any first-class passenger on the line may use this Pullman Car on payment of half-a-crown over and above the ordinary fare for his journey. He may enter or quit the Pullman car at any station where the train stops, but should give notice beforehand of his intention, lest the car should be full. The up train, to which this car is attached, starts from Leeds at 10am, and arrives at King's Cross, London at 2pm. The down train, by which the car returns, leaves King's Cross at 5.30pm, reaching Leeds at 10.10pm. So that a Leeds man, by this arrangement, may start from home after his usual breakfast, fortify himself with lunch at 1 o'clock, take three clear hours for his business in London, dine comfortably at 6 or 7 o'clock, and get to bed in his own house an hour before midnight. This seems to be just what one should want; and it is to be hoped that Manchester and Liverpool men will soon enjoy the same accommodation. We trust that the London & North-Western, the Midland, and the Great Western Railway companies will not delay to follow the example of the Great Northern. Irregular dining hours, beyond all doubt, have shortened the lives of many prosperous and active men of business who were little past middle age. The Pullman Company therefore deserve our support in this department of their enterprise, as well as in the introduction of sleeping cars, which suit the need of a comparatively restricted number of travellers by night. The principal office of the Pullman Palace Car Company in London is situated in the Midland Railway Station, St Pancras, Euston Road. Mr J. Miller is secretary; Mr H. S. Roberts, manager for England, and Mr A. Rapp mechanical superintendent. We are informed that only one dining-car has yet been constructed for use in this country, and it has been under repairs for a day or two in the present week. It may be expected that this convenience will hereafter be universally applied to our railway passenger traffic.'

F. S. Williams observed 'the comfort of this mode of passing the time appears to be appreciated by passengers', which proved to be somewhat of an understatement in view of the rapid growth in this type of service to the public in a relatively short period of time.

The Engineer for 24 October 1879 gave the bill of fare available aboard this first dining car as 'a choice of dishes . . . including soups, fish, entrees, roast joints, puddings and such for dessert. After dining the passenger may walk into the smoking area to take his coffee and cigar'.

During 1879 the position regarding hot boxes on Pullmans improved steadily so that by July of the total number of cases reported (35) only two involved Pullmans whereas the previous year there had been 75 of which 19 had been Pullmans. By the following month with 27 cases, only one was a Pullman car which had to be detached.

However, the Midland had other problems with the Westinghouse brake which far outweighed the problems of Pullman hot boxes in relation to the detention of trains. James Allport wrote to the Board expressing his serious concern and recounting the Pullmans' problems thus:

'The detentions of our Scotch trains in consequence of the failure of the continuous brakes on the new joint stock have become so numerous that I feel it necessary to call your attention to the subject.

'These cases, during the past month of July have amounted to 42 . . . a number very much in excess of anything we have previously experienced.

'I need not enter into the controversy which has taken place between the Westinghouse company and our Carriage Department but I feel compelled to ask that some immediate action be taken to remedy the very serious evils we are now subjected to.

'It will be in the recollection of the Directors that we had a very large number of Pullman carriages taken off the trains in consequence of the heating of the axles, and that after considerable discussion it was thought advisable that the Pullman Company should send one of their own men to attend to the repairs of their stock. Since they have been put in order by the Pullman Company's manager there has been a great improvement in their running, only 11 carriages having been detached with hot boxes between 1 January and 31 July 1879, as against 39 for the corresponding period of 1878, and if the period between 1 April and 31 July be taken when it may be assumed the whole of the carriages had been overhauled by the Pullman Company, a still more reliable improvement has taken place, no carriage having been detached during the four months of 1879 as against 23 detached in the same period of 1878.

'This fact suggests to me whether it would not be advisable for the Directors to take a similar course with regard to the Westinghouse Company and allow the fitting up of the Westinghouse brake to be under the supervision of someone whose experience would qualify them for the duty.'

Both the Carriage & Wagon and Locomotive Committee's met the Westinghouse representative to discuss the defects but the latter committee were unanimous in stating that 'in the interests of the Midland Company' it was 'impossible to allow maintenance of brakes to be in any other hands than those of its officers'.

In the event after due consideration, the Board decided in its view that, the most reliable brake was the non-automatic simple type but since they had decided on 6 November 1878 that an automatic action brake be applied thereafter for general use on the Midland Railway, they decided that without making a final decision, Saunders Improved Brake should be used on any trains hereinafter fitted with automatic brakes.

So it came about that Sanders & Bolithe's brakes were fitted to a number of Pullman cars running on the London to Liverpool and Manchester services, whilst the Westinghouse brake remained in use on the 'Scotch' services on vehicles already so fitted.

On 20 May 1879 Rapp's first report was read to the Carriage & Wagon Committee as follows:

'Maintenance of Pullman cars.
    'The following are in good condition:
    'Parlour cars: "Leo", "Britannia", "Mercury", "Apollo", "Saturn", "Juno", "Eclipse", "Ceres", "Alexandra", "Aries".

'Sleeping cars: "Enterprise", "Norman", "Excelsior", "Princess", "Castalia", "Australia", "Midland".

'Repaired since 1 December, 1878: "Excelsior", "Alexandra", "Leo", "St George", "Transit", "Eclipse", "Enterprise", "Norman", "Saturn", "Mercury", "Britannia", "Juno", "Apollo", "Ceres".

'Cars in shops under repair: "Saxon", "Adonis", "Venus", "Minerva", "Vesta", "Victoria".

'Cars requiring to be sent to shops for repairs: "St George", "Transit", "Scotia", "Aurora", "Comet", "Planet", "Jupiter", "Albion".'

On 1 July the question of additional braking power required on Midland Pullman cars was discussed by the same Committee. Eight cars had been extensively altered in 1877 at a cost of £1,367 with a view to making them suitable for main line traffic. However, these alterations were found 'not to answer and therefore were taken off again'. It was now considered that there was not sufficient hand brake power and alterations at £8 15s (£8.75) per car, of £70 in total, were needed. This was agreed to.

On 3 December 1879 the chairman of the Midland Board, Edward Shipley Ellis, died, having been a member of that body for nearly 23 years, and chairman of it since May 1873. He was succeeded by Matthew William Thompson who was appointed on 17 February 1880, with Timothy Kenrick as his deputy.

Below:
The ornate interior of this drawing room car, 'Albion' clearly indicates the exceptional standards of finish and luxury. Each of the arm-chairs could be independently swivelled to any position, but this type of open layout did not find a ready acceptance among the travelling public. *Author's Collection*

6 New Cars, Conversions and a Tragedy

Construction of Pullman cars in Derby recommenced in 1880 with the erection of two sleeping cars 'Columba' and 'Iona' for the Great Northern Railway. These cars were of somewhat different construction to earlier cars in that their roofs were lined with polished wood rather than the quilted American cloth used before. They were of the standard outward appearance, but slightly shorter having a body length of 50ft 6in and an overall length of 56ft 9in. The four wheeled bogies, with a wheelbase of 8ft, were set at 35ft centres. As new the cars were sent direct from Derby to the GNR and were put to work on the East Coast route to Scotland, replacing the older cars 'Ocean' and 'Germania' which were withdrawn from service and sent to Italy to reinforce the Pullman stock working the 'Indian Mail' train service between Bologna and Brindisi, for which section of line the Pullman Company had an exclusive contract for the provision of sleeping cars.

'Columba' and 'Iona' joined the 1876 car 'India' on the East Coast Joint Stock services between London and Scotland until the latter was wrecked in the Manor House collision on the North Eastern near Thirsk on 2 November, and subsequently scrapped. 'Iona' survived a collision at Northallerton on 4 October 1894 and joined 'Columba' as part of ECJS Nos 232 and 233 respectively, being purchased (one each) by the North Eastern and the Great Northern Companies.

The two were displaced by new sleeping cars and in 1901 became GNR No 2992 ('Iona') and NER No 2966 ('Columba'). The GNR converted No 2992 into a dining saloon with two sections seating 16 and 4 respectively with a small kitchen and pantry at one end which also had a corridor gangway connection. No 2966 was similarly converted by the NER in 1902 into a refreshment car, the work being carried out at York, with a different internal layout. In addition to the main saloon there was a small smoking compartment, a kitchen with a cooking stove and other conveniences, a lavatory and a cupboard for passengers' luggage. The car, still on its original bogies, was finished in the standard NER livery. Only first class passengers were normally catered for, but the third class passenger was admitted on payment of a supplement of 2s 6d (12½p). The car ran in services between Leeds and Scarborough as a breakfast car in the morning and a tea car on the later afternoon return journeys. It was downgraded to a third class saloon in 1907 and was frequently used by Newcastle United Football Club when travelling to away matches until its withdrawal from service on 3 November 1910.

GNR No 2992 is believed to have run on Nottingham to Skegness services to provide a buffet and was withdrawn from use on 27 October 1925 and taken to Lincoln where, as a grounded body it served as a Mutual Improvement Class meeting room at the Great Northern motive power depot for many years. It was finally broken up about 1970.

(Much of the foregoing information is drawn from Ken Hoole's article 'The first British dining car — a case of mistaken identity' in the *Railway World* September 1979 issue.)

On the Midland the original parlour car 'Victoria' was withdrawn and sent by Pullman to the London and South Western Railway after having been remodelled into an open saloon parlour car with 34 seats as against its original arrangement of 17 armchairs and a private room. Arriving on the L&SWR it was renamed 'Alexandra' (the third to be so named!) and was put to work the 11am Pullman car train from Waterloo to Exeter. This car remained in traffic until about 1882 when Behrend says it was put into store. The train became nicknamed 'the Alexandra', and so was known long after the car was no longer in the formation. It is recorded that the Pullman car service did not attract travellers and this may well account for its short life on the line. The British public, it may be observed, were none too impressed with Mr Pullman's parlour cars, popular though they may have been in the wide open spaces of America!

On 1 June 1880 the parlour car services between London and Edinburgh were re-introduced for the summer and autumn and ran until 1 November, one month longer than was normal, as did the London-Perth sleeping car services which began running again on 21 July.

The practice of running these trains only between 1 June and 1 November each year became a regular one. However, the Leeds, Bradford, Manchester and Liverpool portions of the 'Scotch' day express, in both up and down directions, ran after 1 November to and from Carlisle as independent trains.

1881 was marked by heavy snow falls and from Thursday evening, 3 March until the Monday morning, 7 March, the Settle & Carlisle line of the Midland was completely blocked by snow and for the first time the Pullman services along with others ran via Ingleton and the London & North Western Railway as far as Carlisle.

F. S. Williams reported the event thus:

'... on Thursday 3 March 1881, a snow-storm began to fall in West Yorkshire, Westmorland, and around. So furious, in those higher elevations, was the wind, that it rocked the trains, even heavy Pullman carriages, as they paused at stations on the Settle and Carlisle line; and it swept the snow from the upper parts of the great fells "as clean as a broom". "During the day," said the engineer, "we kept the line open, but by 10 o'clock at night the drifts entirely blocked the up road. We then worked the traffic for a short distance on the down line, till an engine, which had been taken from its train to make a run at the drift, bedded itself so fast in the snow that it could not back out. From that time till Sunday morning it was a continual fight with the drifts to try to keep the line clear. Two engines with a gang of nearly 600 men left Dent, and cut the drifts before them to Dent Head, and on their return had at once to repeat the process in order to get back, the drifts of snow filling every gully and cutting to a depth of 30ft. During Saturday night it alternately rained and froze, so that the surface of the snow became firm and frozen; and on Sunday morning when the gale ceased the masses of snow would bear." A contemporary engraving indicates the actual condition of affairs, showing all that was to be seen of an entire train, namely the top of the engine funnel, the snow around being hard. One man who walked over the train found the chimney top convenient as a spittoon. Meanwhile the moisture that had accumulated on the telegraph wires had become as thick as a man's wrist. The lamp-posts on the platform at Dent were buried in the snow. After the line was reopened, a train of 10 locomotives that had "gone cold" — the trains of which had already been removed by fresh engines — was dug out of a drift 30 or 40ft deep and drawn away.'

The Board met on 3 May 1881 to discuss the Pullman Agreement and resolved that it remain in force subject to six months' notice on either side, and subject also to the following definition on the clause under which the Midland Company were to afford facilities to the Pullman Company 'on reasonable terms' for the erection or alteration of carriages either for the Midland or any other company, but not so as to interfere with the use of the shops for the repair of Midland carriages, to operate from 1 August 1881.

The rent of the two sheds at Derby, including rates and taxes and maintenance of buildings and permanent way by the Midland Railway was to be taken at £425 per annum, the cost of gas, water, fuel and other stores to be as per consumption. The actual salary and expenses of Mr Monck and his successor and of clerkage was to be ascertained and the total expenditure was to be considered as joint expenses and borne by the Midland Company and the Pullman Company in proportion to the work done for them respectively in the shops.

On 3 August 1881 the MR Board discussed the Pullman Agreement yet again, after the first three years of its operation and agreed that it should remain in force for a further six months. It was also agreed to accept into traffic two new additional sleeping cars, constructed on the latest improvement, and that the Company agree to two of the present day cars being converted into dining cars at the cost of the Pullman Company, and that Mr Clayton be requested to value the Pullman day cars at present in the possession of the Company and report to the Board.

These two new sleeping cars were named 'St Mungo' and 'St Andrew' and were placed in service on 1 February 1883. These were shorter sleeping cars than the standard type, being only 50ft 6in long in the body and 56ft 9in overall. The two four wheeled bogies, on an 8ft wheelbase were centred at 35ft. These two cars were almost identical with 'Columba' and 'Iona' built for the GNR in 1880.

The new cars replaced two of the older Midland cars 'Castalia' and 'Australia' which were sent to Italy in the spring of 1883. Rather than send these cars all the way empty and pay for the privilege, the Pullman Company collaborated with Thomas Cook & Son Ltd for the provision of a special train in connection with the Italian Fine Arts Exhibition in Rome.

The passengers left London on Friday 23 February 1883 and joined the cars at Calais from where they could travel all the way to Rome arriving on the Sunday evening at 7.15pm. The single first class fare for the whole trip was £10 16s 9d (£10.88) the snag being that no return trip was arranged! Full details of this agreement-violating train are given in George Behrend's excellent book *Pullman in Europe*.

Clayton duly submitted his report on 5 October as follows:
'Estimate of original cost £1,640 each for 14 cars=£22,960, but as the cars have been in traffic upon the average five years and two months each I estimate their present value at £1,301 each, being £18,214 in aggregate.'

It was resolved that Mr Noble, the General Manager, continue his negotiations with Mr Pullman in this matter with a view to the Midland Company purchasing all the cars

Above:
Midland dining saloon car No 15, formerly named 'Windsor', as rebuilt in July 1882 from the original parlour car 'Britannia' assembled at Derby in June 1874 and seen here at Derby in 1902.
Crown Copyright Midland Railway Official photograph courtesy National Railway Museum

Below:
Derby works and station c1885 with the Pullman Car 'sheds' bottom right where all the cars were assembled, repaired and in some cases rebuilt. Note the lifting gantry for de-bogieing the cars and the bogie frames stacked outside. The North Staffordshire Railway locomotive shed is to the left and behind the cameraman.
Midland Railway Official

outright. The 14 cars in question were 'Jupiter', 'Saturn', 'Mercury', 'Juno', 'Venus', 'Vesta', 'Minerva', 'Planet', 'Albion', 'Comet', 'Apollo', 'Aurora', 'Eclipse' and 'Alexandra'.

The two day or parlour cars being converted, and not included in this list, were the oldest parlour cars still on the Midland, namely 'Britannia' and 'Leo'. The conversion work included provision of buffet facilities which increased the weight of the cars to over 27 tons. Six wheeled Pullman type bogies were provided to improve riding and the vehicles were put into traffic as follows: 'Leo' renamed 'Delmonico' in April 1882; 'Britannia' renamed 'Windsor' in July 1882; 'Delmonico' was so named after a famous New York Swiss-born restaurateur of the time, and followed the naming of Pullman's first dining car for use on the Chicago & Alton Railroad, which carried the same name tribute. They were put into service on the 5pm express from London (St Pancras) to Liverpool and the 4.05pm from Liverpool to London as from 10 July 1882.

These trains consisted of three Pullman cars, one of which was an ordinary Pullman drawing-room or 'parlour' car, the second was one of the new dining cars mentioned above with a small kitchen area capable of providing a dinner for forty persons, whilst the third is described by Williams as 'a smaller, but handsomely fitted car run expressly for the occasion'.

The Railway Review issue of 14 July 1882 reported on their introduction as follows:

'A trial trip was made on Friday with the two new Pullman dining room cars named the "Delmonico" and the "Windsor" which this week will commence to run on the Midland line. The "Venus" drawing room car, which has been in use for some time, was also attached to the train. The train left St Pancras shortly after 2 o'clock reaching Leicester at 20 minutes past 4 and returning to the terminus before 7. Among the party on board the cars were Mr M. W. Thompson, Chairman of the Company, Mr John Noble, the General Manager, and Mr F. M. Needham, Superintendent of the Line. The Pullman Car Company was represented by Mr H. S. Roberts, Manager, Mr J. Miller, Secretary, Mr J. Monck, Mechanical Supt, and General H. Porter, Vice-President of the Pullman Car Company of America.

'The cars, which were built under the supervision of Mr Monck at the Pullman Works at Derby, are 58ft long, and 9ft 10in in width. Each dining car seats 21 passengers while 27 may be accommodated in the drawing room car. In the dining car the tables are arranged at right angles to the windows, with a gangway down the centre. The sides and ceiling are inlaid with mahogany panels decorated with paintings of fruit and leaves, while mirrors are abundant and give a greater sense of space. The seats are upholstered in claret plush and overlaid with hand-worked antimacassars, the floor is covered with Wilton carpet and the blinds are of tapestry. Passengers can summon the waiter by an electric bell without moving from their seats. At one end of the car is a smoking room and lavatory, while at the other end is the pantry and the kitchen. The cooking is done on the journey in a range comprising a grill and which, small as its compass, can prepare a dinner for 40 persons. The staff for each car will consist of a conductor, page and cook. The drawing room car has its sides and ceiling inlaid with black walnut and it is provided with a number of swing chairs upholstered in crimson plush. Tables are placed at the sides so that dinner can be served here in case of emergency. A smoking room, a private apartment for the use of a family, and

48

lavatory accommodation are attached to this car. The materials for these cars were brought from Detroit and put together at the Derby workshops of the Pullman Company.

'On the trial trip, dinner cooked on the journey was served in the cars with most satisfactory results. The menu, which comprised six courses, beginning with soup and ending with dessert, was as admirably prepared as at a hotel. The trial trip gave promise of the dining cars proving very popular on the Midland line. On and after 10 July 1882 a Pullman dining saloon car will be attached to the express trains leaving London (St Pancras) for Manchester and Liverpool at 5pm and Liverpool (Central) at 4.5pm and Manchester Central at 4.50pm for London. A table d'hote dinner will be served in the car at 6pm on the down and up journeys, the price of which will be 3s 6d (17½p), exclusive of wines, etc. Passengers can obtain which wines they require for dinner by giving their orders to the conductor prior to the departure of the train, who will obtain them from the refreshment room.

'Special notice to Manchester passengers:

"Manchester passengers by the 4.50pm express are advised that, owing to the limited number of seats in the Pullman dining car, it is desirable to engage their seats as much in advance as possible. This can be done by notifying the stationmaster at the Central Station, Manchester before 3pm, so as to allow time to reserve seats at Liverpool by telegram. Parties of four or five desiring to dine together can be accommodated with special tables by giving notice in advance." '

On 2 August 1882, the MR Board discussed the traffic between the capital and Liverpool and the possibility of providing a 'Limited Pullman Car Train'. The General Manager was asked to discuss conditions for such a train with George Pullman.

More Pullman parlour cars were released by the Midland in October 1881 when 'Ariel', 'Adonis', and 'Ceres', all modified at Derby and provided with an electric lighting system, were transferred to the London Brighton & South Coast Railway to be renamed 'Louise', 'Victoria' and 'Maude' respectively after the Royal Families children. This extension of the use of electricity for lighting followed on the experiment with the first LB&SCR car 'Beatrice' which had had such equipment fitted following its transfer from the Midland in June 1878. Such a system had undoubtedly been a success so far as the LB&SCR were concerned.

On 4 October 1881, Rapp reported to the Carriage & Wagon Committee that he was required in America to superintend the new works of the Pullman Palace Car Company in Chicago and would be returning in six weeks' time. He recommended as his successor Mr Joseph Monck, who had come from the workshops of the Pullman Car Company in America to assist in erecting cars with Mr Rapp, and who had been his principle foreman for two years. Rapp recommended his salary should be £225 per annum. As a matter of interest, Monck is credited with the invention of oval buffer heads to prevent buffer locking on Pullman vehicles in 1883.

General Manager Noble had reported on 16 May 1882 that the Pullman Company was not prepared to sell any of their day or night cars or consent to a reduction in the charges, but they were willing to relieve the Midland Company of one of the day cars 'Jupiter', and this was accordingly released and transferred to the London, Chatham & Dover line. In addition they were willing to make the Pullman day cars more attractive by allowing the Midland to introduce buffets into them at which refreshments could be sold as recorded earlier, but clearly the Midland were determined not to be put off, as we shall see.

Noble had pointed out strongly to Mr Pullman the unfairness of the arrangement under which the Great Northern Company were allowed to run Pullman sleeping cars between London and Scotland without being put under the same restrictions as the Midland Company with regard to the running of other sleeping cars on the line. As a result, Pullman suggested that one solution of the difficulty would be that he should be allowed to furnish to the Midland Company 'a somewhat inferior description of sleeping car for the use of which the same fares might be charged as are charged by the Great Northern and London & North Western companies'. He added that 'four of such cars are now being built in the shops at Derby'. Two of these cars were duly accepted by the Midland and put into service on 30 June 1883, being named 'St Louis' and 'St Denis' and were identical to two other cars completed at the end of 1882, named 'Balmoral' and 'Culross' which had been sent direct to the Great Northern Railway on 2 January 1883.

These cars were not of full Pullman outline, being only 36ft 3in long, with no end platforms and entrance doors set in the middle of the sides of the car.

Their construction had been a speculative venture by Pullman, who hoped to run them on the Ouest Railway of France between Paris and Trouville (which accounts for the name 'St Denis', headquarters of the said railway). He had therefore, found a convenient way of disposing of them, non-standard though they were!

Their internal arrangements are as shown in the diagram (see Appendix 5) and comprised a central vestibule 4ft 6in wide, with external doors each side, in half the width of which were housed on one side the standard Baker car heater and on the other a luggage locker and coal box. A curtained off single Pullman 6ft long cross section sleeping compartment was placed each side of the vestibule with an upper bunk either side and a pair of facing seats below converting to a lower berth for night-time use. Beyond these lay a pair of 3ft 6in wide compartments with a water closet on one side of the gangway and an open lavatory unit on the other. At each end of the vehicle lay a further Pullman cross section sleeping compartment.

As originally built these cars were provided with six wheeled underframes built by the Midland Railway in the Derby carriage works as lot 72 ordered on 25 January 1882. It is clear however, that the vehicles did not ride very well on their 3ft 7in diameter wheels and Stretton records that before they went into service working daily on the Midland's through night service to Greenock from 1 July 1883, the cars were modified by the provision of two four wheeled bogies to improve their riding.

The cars were later used on the service from St Pancras to Stranraer in connection with the steamer services to Larne, but they did not remain on the route for very long since the business was insufficient to recoup the company for the outlay involved.

The two cars on the Great Northern Railway ran between King's Cross and Edinburgh, but proved unpopular and in 1885 were transferred to the Highland Railway to work on the night trains leaving Inverness at 10pm and arriving in Perth at 7am, with a supplement of five shillings (25p) for the privilege. 'Balmoral' retained its name, but 'Culross' was renamed 'Dunrobin'. The service was extended all the way to Glasgow (Buchanan Street) from 7 March 1904 and the cars remained in regular service until 1907 when they were placed in reserve. By 1918 they were stored out of

Above:
One of the two short sleeping cars, 'St Denis', which Pullman provided in 1883 as an 'inferior type of car' so that the Midland could match the fares charged by their competitors — the Great Northern and the LNWR.
Leicester Libraries, Author's Collection

Below:
The destruction of the 'Enterprise' in the fire at Hunslet, Leeds, on 29 October 1882.

use and eventually purchased by Mr F. Marks, who had them moved to Seaford, Sussex, where they were turned into a bungalow. Mr Marks was incidentally the son of Mr J. S. Marks who had just at that time retired from service as the Pullman Car Company's Staff and Rolling Stock Superintendent. Some of the seats from these later found a use in a Brighton public house from where they were purchased by C. Hamilton Ellis and passed to the Curator of Historical Relics at Clapham, John Scholes.

As to the Midland pair their later history will be told in due course, but by 1890 they were already converted to picnic cars.

Shortly before 2am on Sunday 29 October 1882 the 9.15pm down night 'Scotch' express left Normanton heading towards its next stop at Skipton, and included in its formation were two Pullman sleeping cars, 'Enterprise' on its way to Edinburgh and 'Excelsior' bound for Glasgow in the care of Conductors Robert Donaldson and Andrew Baillie respectively. Approaching Hunslet the driver heard the whistle of the safety cord apparatus and, looking back, saw a light above one of the cars and immediately brought the train to a halt near Hunslet South Junction signalbox. Baillie, from one of the vacant berths in his car, also observed a light, reflected in the headboards of his Pullman and, looking out, saw to his horror that the 'Enterprise' was on fire. He rushed out on to the end platform of his car but found that the end door on the Edinburgh vehicle was shut, so he pulled the communication cord on his car and then roused all his passengers.

He assisted in uncoupling the 'Enterprise' from the rest of the train and tried with others to extinguish the fire in the vehicle's roof, by now well alight, with buckets of such water as was available.

Meanwhile his colleague, Donaldson, in the affected car, had been having quite a night already, having had to deal with a Dr Arthur who had unsteadily walked down the platform at St Pancras in an apparent state of intoxication before getting into the front part of the train and who, upon arrival at Leicester, had moved into the Edinburgh car and asked for a brandy and soda. Donaldson had diplomatically said he only had soda water left, whereupon the Doctor had taken a bottle of it and added it to a concoction of his own which he had described as 'Egyptian brandy'. The conductor had then removed the Doctors' shoes and a cigar which he had been attempting to light, and, after asking for his overcoat, Arthur had apparently gone to sleep.

When the fire had broken out there had been four passengers in the car, a Mr Dove who had left via the end door, a Mr Main who had broken a window in berth No 5 and had been pulled to safety and a Mr Cranston in berth No 8, who had boarded the train at Sheffield and gone to bed with a ready lamp burning. Donaldson had pointed out the danger of such a practice, although not strictly against Pullman rules, and had advised him to be sure to extinguish it before going to sleep. Cranston and Donaldson differed in their accounts of the next series of events, but Cranston escaped.

In an attempt to douse the flames the car was first moved 876yd down the line to a water crane but the hose would not reach the roof so it was pushed back a few yards to a hose which had been run out from Nicholson's Chemical Works and there the fire was eventually put out.

A short time later two police officers went into the charred remains of the car and made the grim discovery of the remains of Dr Arthur in berth No 7. Colonel Yolland conducted the official enquiry and concluded that the fire had resulted from Cranston's reading lamp setting fire to the blind in his berth. Dr Arthur probably succumbed to the smoke and fumes whilst in his inebriated state before the flames reached him. Colonel Yolland's main criticism was however levelled at the driver for bringing the train to an immediate stand rather than proceeding to Hunslet station where the fire could have been efficiently tackled and Arthur's life possibly saved.

The Harrison communication cord, of a pattern not approved by the Board of Trade, also came in for some criticism in that it could only be reached from the platforms of the cars. In this instance the opening of the end doors to get at the cord had so increased the passage of air through the car as to give the fire a complete hold on the vehicle.

A claim for £2,489 8s 1d (£2,489.40$\frac{1}{2}$) was laid against the Midland for the costs of restoring the damage done to the car, and the Midland Board agreed to pay this amount to the Pullman Company at their meeting on 16 March 1883. The sleeping car was in fact written off and scrapped, for Pullman suggested on 1 February 1884 that instead of rebuilding the car a new sleeping car, somewhat different in interior fittings, and still in the Derby shops, be substituted in lieu, since the Pullman Company had no other use for it. This was agreed and the sleeping car 'Missouri' was accepted into service the same month.

'Missouri' was one of two cars that Monck had reported as complete and standing in the shops on 5 October 1883, the other one being 'Michigan' which stayed unused in the shed until May 1886 when finally accepted into stock by the Midland.

The damage to 'Enterprise' was not the only fire on board a Pullman in 1882, for earlier on 11 February, and also by coincidence at Leeds, the Great Northern dining car 'Prince of Wales' also took alight, although in this case the damage was fortunately confined to the main saloon. The car was returned to Derby and repaired at a cost of £500.

Below:
The interior of 'Iona' or 'Columba' whilst snowed up on the North Eastern on 1 March 1886 at Acklington, some 12 miles north of Morpeth as captured by a local photographer. The conductor is providing welcome drinks for the stranded passengers. *C. B. Foster*

7 Parlour and Sleeping Cars Purchased

Returning to the Midland services again — on 1 May 1883 an improved service was provided from St Pancras to Liverpool, the portion of express trains for that city running direct, via Skelton Junction, rather than via Manchester (Central) Station, as they had since 1880. The Liverpool portion of some trains ran separately to Derby, the 12 noon from London for instance running all the way from there to Liverpool, a distance of $91\frac{1}{2}$ miles, without any intermediate stop, the fastest trains doing the trip in 5hr 10min. The Pullman dining cars ran to and from Manchester, rather than Liverpool, leaving both there and the capital city at 5pm.

By 5 October 1883 the Midland Board had decided on a definite purchase of the Pullman day cars, 15 in number then being in service, and authorised the General Manager to conclude an agreement with George Pullman on the basis of a payment of £1,600 for the purchase of each car plus an amount to be ascertained being the net cost expended on the conversion of the two parlour cars into dining cars. Clearly this time the Board intended to have its way.

General Manager Noble was obviously successful in his negotiations with George Pullman for the following announcement appeared in the newspapers at the end of October 1883:

'Midland Railway

'On and from 1 November 1883 Passengers holding First Class Tickets will be allowed to ride in the Pullman Day Cars Without Extra Payment. These Cars run daily between London (St Pancras) and Liverpool, Manchester, Carlisle, and Glasgow, respectively, and are warmed during the winter months. A special Attendant accompanies them, and they are fitted with Lavatory accommodation.

'Dining Cars are attached to the 5.0pm train from London (St Pancras) to Manchester, Liverpool, &c, and to the 5.0pm train from Manchester to London (St Pancras), into which Passengers from Liverpool &c, can change at Derby. No extra charge beyond the sum payable for the dinner will be made.

John Noble,

Derby, October 1883
General Manager'

The Pullman supplement was thus removed, and all first class passengers could now avail themselves of the comforts of these cars. The payment of this supplement was always a matter of some objection to passengers in Britain, whilst being more readily accepted in America.

On 20 December 1883 the Carriage & Wagon Committee considered the Traffic Committee's minute of 7 December, which reported Mr Clayton calling attention to the necessity of doing repairs to the Pullman dining cars at as early a date as possible, and a plan was submitted showing how one of the cars, which are known as the Midland Pullmans (ie the Midlands own day cars of 1874) might be converted into a dining car at a cost of £716 so that it could be available as a spare dining car during the necessary repairs to the other cars. The conversion was agreed to and it was suggested that the work be carried out at the earliest possible date, the scheme receiving General Purposes Committee approval. By 4 January 1884 Monck was able to report that first class day car number 8 had been remodelled as a dining car, and that minor repairs had been done to first class Midland car No 5, one of the three remaining.

Monck's report given to the Carriage & Wagon Committee on 4 July 1884 is worth recording and was as follows:

'Good condition:
  Midland cars first class 5 and 6
                third class 2
Since 1 April 1884 Midland car No 1 (sic) remodelled into dining car 'London'.
3rd class car No 2 and 1st class car No 6 repainted.
Under repairs:
  3rd class car No 1
Requiring repairs:
  1st class car No 7
3rd class cars Nos 3 and 4.'

There were changes in the services between London and Manchester on 1 July 1884 from which date the 3.30pm down and the 11.55am and 3.30pm up from Manchester to London was to run between Manchester and Leicester without stopping, by-passing Derby by using the Chaddesden sidings route, the total journey time being cut to 4hr 15min. The 12 noon express ran the same route taking 4hr 20min and the Liverpool portion of the express now linked with the Manchester portion at Leicester.

On 17 July the Carriage & Wagon Committee were again discussing the question of dining cars, which had obviously been a successful venture, and it was decided that the General Purposes Committee be asked to agree to the conversion of two more cars known as the Midland Pullmans being converted into dining cars 'that they may run between St Pancras and Leeds'. This was duly agreed to at a cost of £1,580.

Monck's very full report of 3 October 1884 gave the position then as follows:

'Good condition:
  Parlour cars: "Aurora", "Apollo", "Mercury", "Planet", "Saturn", "Vesta", "Albion", and "Minerva".
  Dining cars: "Delmonico", "Windsor", and No 17 (late No 7), "London".
  Midland cars: First class No 5
               Third class Nos 1, 2, 3 and 4.
  Sleeping cars: "Excelsior", "Missouri", "Norman", "Saxon", "Scotia", "St Mungo", "St Andrew", "St Louis", "St Denis", "Transit", "Princess", "St George".
  Repaired since 1 July 1884:
  Parlour cars: "Albion" and "Minerva".

Dining cars: "Delmonico", and No 15 (late "Windsor") and No 7 (remodelled into No 17).
Midland cars: 3rd class Nos 1, 3 and 4
Sleeping cars: "Princess" and "St George".
Now under repair:
Parlour car: "Eclipse".
Midland car: No 6 (to be remodelled to dining car No 18)
Requiring repairs:
Parlour cars: "Venus", "Alexandra", "Comet" and "Juno".
Sleeping car: "Midland".'

From 1 October 1884 Pullman day cars began running on some of the expresses between Bradford and London (St Pancras) and dining cars were included in the trains running at 5.30pm from St Pancras and 4.55pm from Bradford providing a full evening dinner service during the journey.

With the introduction of the summer services on 1 July 1885 an improved 'Scotch' night service, the 'Highland Express', ran at 8.25pm from St Pancras to Leicester without a stop in 2hr 2min, and in the opposite direction at 5.08am ex-Leicester in the same time, arriving in St Pancras at 7am. This train also ran from Carlisle to Keighley without stopping, and the improvements were considered to be necessary in opposition to the London and North Western Railway services which were all accelerated and included a night 'Scotch Mail' running without passengers for the first time.

From the end of the summer season, 1 October saw the continuation of the Pullman sleeping car and a carriage service all the way from St Pancras, which it left at 8.25pm, to Stranraer, although there was no communication with North British Railway services.

On 4 December 1885 the Carriage & Wagon Committee considered the existing lighting of the Pullman cars and decided that, with the agreement of the Pullman Company, all the sleeping cars would be fitted up with Pintsch's compressed gas light fittings.

The dining cars in service proved very popular and pressure of custom required the Carriage & Wagon Committee to consider increasing the kitchen accommodation of the five dining cars at a cost of £290. The cars were 'Delmonico', 'Windsor', 'London', 'No 17' and 'No 18'. In the event only one car was altered at a cost of £58 at the request of the Traffic Committee.

A modification to two cars 'From Plan 129 to plan 129A' was reported by Monck to the Carriage & Wagon Committee on 2 July 1886. These were 'Michigan' and 'Missouri', the last two sleeping cars to be built at the Derby shops. These were somewhat shorter sleepers than the earlier standard, being only 49ft 3in over the body. It will be remembered that 'Missouri' had been taken into stock in February 1884 to replace the ill-fated car 'Enterprise', but 'Michigan' had been standing in the shops since completion in September 1883. She was eventually accepted by the Midland in May 1886 along with 'Missouri' for use on the Midland Services to Scotland, alongside the even smaller sleeping cars 'St Louis' and 'St Denis'.

However, the Midland were at last beginning to think about the kind of sleeping carriage they ought to put into service after the agreement with Pullman expired in February 1888 and the Carriage & Wagon Committee asked, on 1 October 1886, that

Above:
Three Pullman parlour car are in this empty stock train headed by Johnson 0-6-0 No 1365 near Hellifield about 1900. *LGRP (12179) courtesy David & Charles*

Below:
Interior of St Pancras station about 1887 with a Pullman sleeping car at the head of the nearest rake of coaches. *Courtesy British Railways*

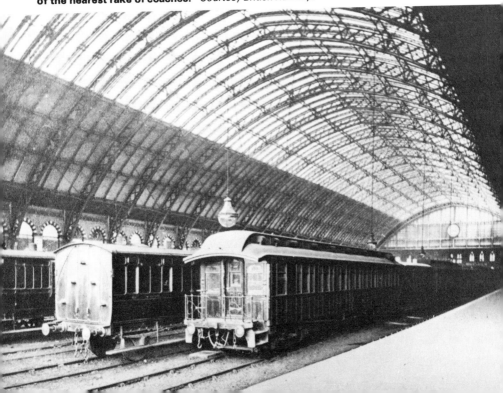

designs be prepared for the Midland's own sleeping cars. On 17 March 1887 Clayton placed the five designs before the Committee which approved the construction of one carriage of each of three types, namely:

Plan 1 48ft sleeping carriage to cost £900
Plan 2 Not adopted
Plan 3 54ft sleeping carriage to cost £1,300
Plan 4 Not adopted
Plan 5 32ft sleeping carriage to cost £650

One of each was approved for building during 1887 at the Carriage & Wagon meeting of 1 April 1887.

With the introduction of the summer timetable on 1 July 1887 further changes in services ensued. The up and down day 'Scotch' expresses stopped at Bedford, the time taken being made up in running, and the service to Edinburgh with a day parlour car recommended. A new express was inaugurated leaving London (St Pancras) at 2pm and ran to Manchester via Nottingham, Radford, Butterley and Ambergate (North Junction), stopping at Kettering, Nottingham and Miller's Dale only. This was the first time that a Midland fast express train had been scheduled to run over the Butterley route between Codnor Park Junction and Crich Junction.

At the change to winter timetables in October 1887 the stops at Bedford and Luton for the up and down 'Scotch' expresses were only made as required.

On 18 February 1888 the agreement with Pullman in respect of the sleeping cars came to an end, and, a new agreement not having been made, the cars were withdrawn for two weeks from all sleeping car traffic.

The Carriage & Wagon Committee were probably relieved to have the following letter placed before them at their meeting of 15 March 1888:

'From John Noble, General Manager.

10 March 1888

Dear Sirs,

We have purchased the 14 Pullman Sleeping Cars now running on the Midland line and are under an obligation to take off the Pullman name. I shall be glad if you will do so and substitute the word "Midland" for it, also re-number the cars and removing the names "St Mungo" etc by which they are at present known.

Yours truly,

John Noble'

It was ordered that this be carried out, and the names were obliterated, the cars being renumbered in the series 20-33, the 'Pullman' name on the cant-rail panel being replaced by the word 'Midland'. The list of cars renumbered is as follows:

No	Old Name	No	Old Name	No	Old Name	No	Old Name
20	'Excelsior'	24	'Transit'	28	'St Andrew'	32	'Missouri'
21	'Midland'	25	'Saxon'	29	'St Mungo'	33	'Michigan'
22	'St George'	26	'Scotia'	30	'St Louis'		
23	'Princess'	27	'Norman'	31	'St Denis'		

By this date the renumbering of the parlour cars had also been similarly completed in order of building as follows:

No	Old Name	No	Old Name
1	'Saturn'	8	'Albion'
2	'Juno'	9	'Comet'
3	'Mercury'	10	'Apollo'
4	'Venus'	11	'Aurora'
5	'Minerva'	12	'Alexandra'
6	'Vesta'	13	'Eclipse'
7	'Planet'		

Those parlour cars and first class day cars which had been rebuilt as hotel or dining cars took the remaining numbers thus:

No	Old Name or Number	No	Old Name or Number
14	'Leo', renamed 'Delmonico'	17	7
15	'Britannia', renamed 'Windsor'	18	6
16	8 renamed 'London'		

These vehicles all had six wheeled bogies fitted when rebuilt. The sole unconverted first class Midland day car No 5 is believed to have become No 19 to complete the number series.

As to the old third class baggage day cars numbers 1-4, these were not renumbered and were withdrawn for departmental use about this time, the day cars never having proved very popular with the public.

The ending of the Pullman agreement left Monck without a job, but Clayton reported to the Carriage & Wagon Committee on 4 May 1888 that he had offered the former Pullman shops manager a situation as foreman to look after the maintenance of the parlour and sleeping cars at Derby at a wage of £3 per week, and this had been accepted. Monck later left Derby to work for the Wagons-Lits Company and became the resident inspecting engineer at Brussels supervising the erection of cars being built for that Company at Godarville and Haine St Pierre. He later went on to work for Mr W. S. Laycock, the well known railway contractor and retired to Deal in Kent where he became a publican.

Mr Wildlagen also joined the Compagnie Internationale des Wagons Lits following his departure from the Pullman Company and joined their Operating Department.

The two Pullman car sheds at Derby, where the cars had been erected, rebuilt and maintained, each of which was about 240ft long and 38ft wide, continued in use for maintenance purposes. By 1903 the one nearest to the London Road had been converted into a rifle range for use by the Midland Railway Rifle Club and the second one followed suit in the 1920s for use by the London, Midland & Scottish Railway Rifle Club.

Both sheds have since been demolished the last one being cleared away, along with the remnants of the old North Staffordshire Railway Locomotive shed nearby, in the mid-1960s, to make way for the new power signalbox which now occupies part of the site.

8 Autumnal Days

The beginning of the end for Midland Pullman cars came during the great coal strike of 1893 when train loadings were being drastically reduced in order to conserve valuable fuel supplies. In this respect the Pullman cars represented a very high trailing load per passenger seat figure, and about the middle of September all of the drawing room cars were withdrawn from traffic by the Traffic Committee and placed in the carriage storing shed at Spondon Junction near Derby, which was located at the southern end of the Chaddesden sidings.

Thomas Clayton reported to the Carriage & Wagon Committee on 5 January 1894 that in his opinion they would soon suffer rapid deterioration whilst out of traffic, and he wished to know what to do with them. One car was by then 19-years old, eight cars were 18 years old and four cars over 17-years old. He reported that they had been taken great care of up to that time and the internal cabinet work was still in very good condition, but if they were allowed to remain out of traffic and in the damp, it would soon become in a bad condition as the cabinet work was of 'that description which required to be kept dry and taken care of'.

It was duly resolved as a start to convert eight of the drawing room cars into picnic saloons in accordance with a sketch produced at the Carriage & Wagon Committee meeting on 15 February 1894 at a cost of £520 (£65 each) and the work was charged to the revenue account. These appear to have been numbers 6 ('Vesta'), 7 ('Planet'), 8 ('Albion'), 9 ('Comet'), 10 ('Apollo'), 11 ('Aurora'), 12 ('Alexandra') and 13 ('Eclipse'). Later the same year, on 20 September, the Carriage & Wagon Committee resolved to convert a further four drawing room cars into third class picnic saloons at a revenue cost of £65 each and this work was approved by both the General Purposes and the Traffic Committees.

With the advent of more modern stock, Mr G. H. Turner, the Midlands' General Manager wrote on 24 August 1894, to the Carriage & Wagon Committee stating that five of the Pullman sleeping cars were no longer required for traffic in that capacity and suggested their conversion into saloons for 'using in various kinds of traffic'. The Carriage & Wagon Committee considered this on 2 November and agreed to the matter being passed forward for approval. These appear to have been numbers 20 (formerly 'Excelsior'), 21 ('Midland'), 22 ('St George'), 25 ('Saxon') and possibly 26 ('Scotia'). The two short sleeping cars 30 ('St Denis') and 31 ('St Louis') were also converted to picnic cars around the same time.

As the use of the Pullman cars continued to decline the General Manager submitted a proposal to the Traffic Committee for the conversion of two of the Pullman dining carriages for picnic purposes. It was decided that these should be regarded as renewals

Top:
Drawing room car No 8, formerly 'Albion', is included in this official Midland Railway photograph of a train posed at Castle Donnington behind Johnson 4-4-0 No 1338 about 1891. *Author's Collection*

Above:
Johnson Singles Nos 175 and 127 head a down express near Hendon in 1896 with a train which includes a Pullman sleeping car.
LGRP (21144) courtesy David & Charles

Below:
The photographic register caption for this official view reads 'Pullman car train, Chaddesden sidings' and the formation is identical with the view taken of Johnson 4-2-2 No 27 passing Child's Hill & Cricklewood which appears elsewhere.
Midland Railway Official Author's Collection

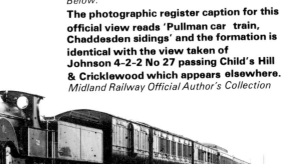

of existing stock and the Carriage & Wagon Committee agreed to this and approved the proposal on 6 May 1898.

On 19 October 1897 George Mortimer Pullman collapsed and died from a stroke in the streets of Chicago at the age of 66 years. Thus passed one of the visionaries of the railway world who had seen a need and made his name universally known in meeting it. After Pullman's death the Company in Britain continued to be run by the trustees of his estate, and Robert Lincoln, son of the assassinated President of the USA, succeeded as head of the American organisation. J. S. Marks continued as head of the British Pullman Palace Car Company, with offices at 26 Victoria Street, Westminster.

The last 'throw of the dice' as it were between the Midland and the Pullman car companies came with the requirement for a further four new sleeping cars of modern design which the Midland Board had considered on 13 August 1897. Considering the matter on 3 February 1899 the Carriage & Wagon Committee hear the report of the General Manager that he had had communications with both the Pullman Car Company and the Wagner Car Company, and that the latter had declined to build the cars. However, the Pullman Company had sent in a specification and were prepared to construct two or four cars at a cost of $15,000 each, subject to certain works affecting brake and bogie gear being carried out by the Midland Company. This work Mr Clayton estimated would cost £345 per vehicle, and facilities for the erection of the cars would also be required at Derby.

It was resolved that an order for four sleeping cars should be placed and the matter was referred to the General Purposes Committee who gave it their approval on 3 March.

The cost of the cars proved a little higher than the first estimate and the Carriage & Wagon Committee were asked to approve an increase of £150 for each vehicle, bringing the cost to £3,495 each. This was agreed to.

Construction of the cars went ahead and by 6 April 1900 the Committee were told that the cars were complete and ready for traffic. They were numbered in the Pullman car sequence as numbers 34 to 37 and they were introduced in May 1900 in the night express formations from London (St Pancras) to Edinburgh and Glasgow.

These new cars were built to the by then standard Pullman design, modified to suit the British loading gauge, and each had sleeping accommodation for only 11 passengers, this time there being no upper berths. Five of these berths were in separate compartments (two doubles and one single) with access from a side corridor. The remaining six berths were to the standard Pullman lower berth section arrangement consisting of a pair of facing seats convertible into a single berth for night-time use, three of these being placed each side of a central gangway. A gent's toilet was provided at one end together with a small kitchen compartment from which the attendant could supply light refreshments to order, whilst at the other end was a ladies' toilet compartment and a standard Baker car heater enclosure. The vehicle ends were rounded with a vestibule having side entrance doors, but no inter-communication between cars was provided for. Oil gas lighting was fitted with lamps on either side of the clerestory of the roof.

Externally the bodies were finished in narrow strips without panelling and were painted in the standard Midland crimson lake colour, with gold ornamentation and lettering.

The six wheeled bogies were provided by the Midland Company to their standard

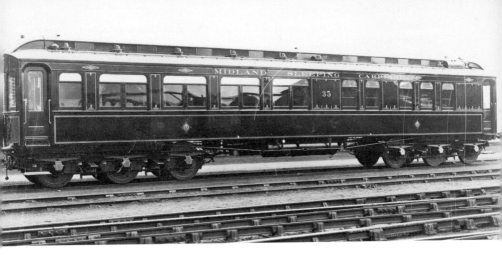

Above:
Official photograph of No 35, one of the last four Pullman sleeping cars to be supplied to the Midland Railway, and placed in service in April 1900.
Crown Copyright Midland Railway Official courtesy National Railway Museum

Below:
Johnson 4-2-2 No 27 heads an express which includes a Pullman parlour car through Child's Hill & Cricklewood station about 1899.
LGRP (22163) courtesy David & Charles

pattern, having a 12ft 6in wheelbase, and all the running and draw gear was also provided by the Midland. Bogie centres were 40ft, overall length was 60ft and overall height was 13ft 1in, the maximum permitted by the Midland loading gauge. Working weight was 33 tons.

In 1905 these sleeping cars were rebuilt with private berths throughout providing one double berth, seven single berths and one smoking compartment. The gent's lavatory and small buffet were retained at the smoking compartment end whilst at the double berth end was the ladies' lavatory and heating compartment as before.

Three of these sleeping cars survived to be taken over by the London, Midland & Scottish Railway Company at its formation on 1 January 1923, becoming numbers 2771, 2772 and 2773, the casualty being old No 35, scrapped before that date. About 1925 they were again renumbered 02771-02773.

The old parlour cars and sleeping cars continued in traffic for a few more years finding use in special excursions, for hire by private parties and as picnic specials.

In 1905 came the conversion of the first of the parlour cars for use in push-pull trainsets as autocars. Order No 3053 was issued on 21 December for the alteration of four Midland and Great Northern Joint Railway 4-4-0 tank locomotives to run with four of the old Pullman parlour cars numbers 1, 2, 5 and 10 on branch lines, the locomotives were numbered 19, 40, 10 and 8 respectively, but by October 1906 engines 40 and 8 had been changed over and the tank engines were renumbered to correspond with the trailer car number.

The units were put to work over the Hemel Hempstead branch and the Derby to Melbourne, Derby to Ripley and Derby to Wirksworth branches.

According to a report in the local newspaper the *Derby and Chesterfield Reporter* ('Trials last Friday') of 9 February 1906 there had been agitation by the inhabitants of Wirksworth, Derbyshire, for a more frequent train service and similar pressures existed elsewhere on the outlying sections of the Midlands' route to Manchester and Sheffield, regarded as 'cul-de-sac' routes.

Below:
Another official view of a 1900 sleeping car, this time of No 36 showing the details of the opposite side. The Midland pattern six-wheeled bogies and all of the running and draw gear were provided by the Derby works.
Crown Copyright Midland Railway Official courtesy National Railway Museum

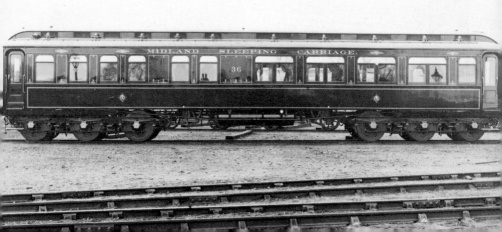

The District Council had been assured by Mr J. Matthieson, General Manager of the Midland, that a reply to the request would shortly be given and on 2 February 1906 the first steam motor with trailer was tried out.

These auto-car sets only conveyed third class passengers and augmented the existing services. Unlike normal branch trains, which often conveyed as many as three or four vans solely to cope with the milk traffic, the units worked entirely on their own.

The remote control equipment 'comprised a wondrous rattle of cables and wires which were conducted through the clerestory roof over the passengers' heads'. Services in the Derby district began with effect from 1 March 1906 and the public handbill announcing the new type of branch trains gave the following information:

Below:
Part of the interior of 1900 Pullman sleeper No 36 showing the washing facilities with the lavatory beyond before the vehicles were altered to private berths throughout in 1905. Note the ornate decoration and the indicator top left.
Crown Copyright Midland Railway Official courtesy National Railway Museum

'The following rail motor service will be in operation on weekdays in addition to the existing service. Third Class Ordinary Fares only will be charged.'

The services are listed below in working format:

Arrive		Depart	Arrive		Depart
	Derby	7.40am	12.22pm	Melbourne	12.38pm
7.56am	Melbourne	8.12am	12.56pm	Derby	1.55pm
8.32am	Derby	8.45am	2.35pm	Melbourne	2.50pm
9.29am	Wirksworth	9.45am	3.25pm	Derby	4.55pm (F.x)
10.18am	Derby	10.32am	5.11pm	Melbourne	5.23pm
11.06am	Ripley	11.25am	5.40pm	Derby	
11.57am	Derby	12.05pm			

A further works order, 3031A, was issued on 21 December 1905 for the fitting of vacuum brake, communication gear and draw gear to one of the five 0-4-0 side tank locomotives, numbers 1528-32, then being built at Derby, in order that it could run with former Pullman parlour car No 3. This work was never carried out however and the order was cancelled on 7 June 1907. One must comment that a tank locomotive of this size might have found working such a heavy old carriage as a Pullman parlour car beyond the limits of both its tractive power and its braking power!

On 3 February 1908 the Midland & Great Northern Joint Railway tanks 2 and 10 were to be fitted with new boilers to order 3442, for continued working on the autocar services, and further alterations were done under Order 3478 (No 2 autocar) and Order 3479 (No 10 autocar), both issued on 28 May 1908.

These motor train sets continued in use until 1912 when the M&GN tank locomotives were returned to their home ground and the three Midland 0-4-4 tanks, numbers 142, 143 and 144, which had been on loan to the M&GN Joint line in lieu, returned to the Midland. As a matter of interest these M&GN tanks were later sold to HM Government in 1917 during World War 1 for use by the War Department.

Below:
Midland autocar set comprising Midland & Great Northern Joint Railway 4–4–0T No 8 and old parlour car No 10, formerly 'Apollo'.
Crown Copyright, Midland Railway Official photograph, courtesy National Railway Musuem

Above:
Autocar train at Wirksworth, Derbyshire, in 1906 comprising Midland & Great Northern Joint 4–4–0 No 10 and ex-parlour car 'Minerva' serving as the trailer.
Real Photographs (72047)

Below:
A Pullman parlour car is the leading vehicle in this Midland motor-train, with a tank locomotive at the centre to provide motive power, as it stands at Ripley station, Derbyshire c1908. *J. Valentine & Sons courtesy D. F. Tee*

9 Pullmans in Retirement

Gradually the Pullmans were phased out of use completely, and by the outbreak of World War 1 in 1914 a large number had already been converted for departmental use or alternatively taken off their bodies and grounded at various locations for use as mess rooms, departmental outdoor offices, storage accommodation, etc.

Not much detailed information on this period has survived, but from various sources it is possible to add the following brief notes.

The original Pullman sleeping car 'Midland', the most travelled of all, which had become No 21 at the renumbering following takeover of the sleeping cars by the Midland Company in February 1888, was grounded on a site near Skipton station in Yorkshire, and turned into a very commodious local Carriage & Wagon Office, mess room and stores. It lay there until June 1970, when in response to an enquiry from Derby Museums in connection with the Midland Railway Project, it was offered for sale at £65.

However, the task of moving it immediately was put off due to the financial implications, and it was not until September 1972 that a new approach was made as to its availability, together with a pair of Pullman bodies lying in the goods yard at Bradford (Forster Square). The offer of the Skipton body was made again, with the two at Bradford being offered at £69 each, and these offers were accepted.

It should be pointed out that at that time a positive identification of the three bodies had not been made. However, by 14 March 1974 when the arrangement had been made to move the Skipton body it had been identified as no less than the original Pullman sleeper 'Midland', and thus its historic significance became even more important. The body travelled by road to Derby on 14-15 March, thus returning to its place of building more than a century afterwards. It was placed in store in the former Normanton Barracks of the Sherwood Foresters Regiment and was finally moved to the Midland Railway Centre on 4 September 1981.

The two Bradford bodies were moved a year later, and with great difficulty over the two days 30 April and 1 May to the Midland Railway Centre site at Butterley station goods yard, near Ripley, Derbys. These have since also proved to be of extreme interest being eventually identified as examples of the two types of the Midlands' own day cars built in 1874 to Pullman outline, to run with Pullman's own cars in the complete Pullman trains of that period. The first class one is probably No 5, the number of the other not having yet come to light. This first class body still shows clear evidence of having been fitted up for push-pull working at some time in its history and still has the remains of an enclosed vestibule at one end.

So happily three bodies are preserved and plans exist to retore at least 'Midland' and possibly the others in due course to make up a most historic Pullman train, mainly for

Above:

The body of the very first sleeping car 'Midland' in use as a Carriage & Wagon office at Skipton on 30 July 1965. It has since been recovered for preservation and is now at the Midland Railway Centre in Derbyshire. *D. F. Tee*

Below:

The other short sleeping car No 30, originally 'St Louis', languishes in the sidings at Heysham in 1905 after withdrawal from service but still on its bogies.
H. C. Casserley

69

static exhibition in the Midland Railway Centre Museum, but also for occasional demonstration use.

Other known Pullman body locations are listed below:

Location	Type
Ashchurch	Part of a body only, still extant in 1974.
Barking	Pullman body until about 1959 (possibly not Midland)
Bath	Pullman sleeping car body still extant in 1930.
Bedford	Third class Midland Pullman style day baggage car body (broken up 1966).
Birmingham	Pullman sleeping car body 'Saxon' and third class day car body until after 1957.
Cheadle Heath	Two Pullman sleeping car bodies until c1960 (one 'St Louis').
Hellifield	Pullman sleeping car body similar to 'Midland', until after 1954.
Heysham	Short Pullman sleeping car 'St Denis' still on bogies in 1905.
Sheffield	Pullman parlour car body.
Tilbury (Riverside)	Pullman parlour car body in use as a messroom. Broken up after 1961.
Tonge & Breedon (Derbys)	Midland 'Pullman' style third class baggage car body. Broken up 1948.

The above list is by no means complete, since in the early part of this century many more such Pullman bodies must have seen similar service as grounded bodies before being finally broken up, so well were they constructed when originally built.

In addition to the above a number of Derby built cars are known to have been converted for other uses after withdrawal and a few examples are given below:

'Albert Edward' a parlour car built at Derby in 1877, which went directly to the London, Brighton & South Coast Railway, was rebuilt with enclosed vestibules about 1889 and electrically lit, was converted to third class car No 4 in 1915 and when taken out of use became a grounded body at Preston Park near Brighton.

'Ariel' a parlour car dating from August 1876, also erected at Derby, was rebuilt there in 1881 as a brake parlour car and transferred to the LB&SCR where it becane 'Louise'. It was condemned on 31 December 1929 and became a bungalow at Selsey.

'Balmoral' and 'Dunrobin', two of the four short sleeping cars; which were built in 1882 at Derby, and were not of the usual Pullman pattern as already noted, after service on both the Great Northern and Highland Railways, were withdrawn in 1918 and placed together at Seaford, Sussex, to form a bungalow dwelling for the son of Mr J. S. Marks who had just retired from service as the Pullman Car Company's Staff & Rolling Stock Superintendent (see earlier in text).

'Iona' erected at Derby in 1880 for the Great Northern Railway, as a sleeping car and later as a dining saloon, saw extensive service on the East Coast main line with the Great Northern and North Eastern Railways before being withdrawn on 27 October 1925. Its body was taken off the bogies at Lincoln where it was in use as a Mutual Improvement Class meeting room for many years, being finally broken up about 1970.

As a final footnote, it is worth recording that long after the Pullman cars had ceased regular working on the routes from London to Manchester, Liverpool, Glasgow and Edinburgh the trains in which they were formerly to be found were often still referred to as the 'Pullmans', even into the 1920s and 1930s. Old habits die hard, and nowhere so hard as in railway lore and operating parlance. Long may their memory survive.

Above:
The grounded body of Midland Pullman outline 1st/2nd day car at Bradford, Forster Square, on 16 May 1971. This body, along with a 3rd/baggage car body was rescued for preservation, and is now at the Midland Railway Centre, Butterley, Derbyshire. *R. H. Offord*

Below:
The two Bradford day car bodies loaded and ready to depart for the Midland Railway Centre on 30 April 1975. *P. Hickling*

Above:
After more than a century of existence the body of the first Pullman sleeper, 'Midland' arrives at her final destination for preservation at the Midland Railway Centre, Butterley, Derbyshire, only a few miles from Derby where she was first assembled and put into service way back in January, 1874. Photograph taken on 21 November 1981. *Midland Railway Trust Collection*

Below:
Original Midland Pullman outline third class/baggage brake body at the Midland Railway Centre, Butterley, in March 1980 in use as an office and store after its timely rescue from destruction at Bradford, and beyond the 1st/2nd composite rescued at the same time. It is hoped to eventually restore it. *Author*

Above:
The only surviving example of a Midland Pullman-outline 1st/2nd composite body in use yet again for messing accommodation at the Midland Railway Centre, Butterley in March 1980 after recovery from Bradford (Forster Square) where it had been for at least half a century. It is hoped that it may eventually be restored. *Author*

Below:
Pullman sleeping car body of early date serving as messing facilities at Hellifield on 23 April 1954. *H. C. Casserley*

Bibliography

Pullman in Europe, George Behrend (Ian Allan, 1962)
Derby Works & Midland Locomotives, J. B. Radford (Ian Allan 1967)
Personal Notebooks of C. E. Stretton (Leicester Libraries)
The Midland Main Line, E. G. Barnes (Allen & Unwin, 1969)
Bradshaws Guide (various dates)
Midland Railway Timetables (various dates)
Our Iron Roads, F. S. Williams (Bemrose & Sons, 1884)
The Midland Railway, F. S. Williams (various editions)
The American Passenger Car, by J. H. White

Other Sources Consulted
Midland Railway Company
Minutes of the Board of Directors
Minutes of the Carriage & Wagon Committee
Minutes of the Finance Committee
Minutes of the Traffic Committee
Minutes of the Way & Works Committee

Great Northern Railway Company
Minutes of the Board of Directors
Miscellaneous papers on Pullman dining and sleeping cars

Railways Blue Book — The Continuous Brake Returns
The Illustrated London News (various issues)
The Engineer (various issues)
Engineering (various issues)
Personal correspondence with A. J. Bower Esq, of Solihull, Warwicks

Appendices

1 Pullman Cars Erected at Derby 1874 to 1883 and 1900

Original Name or Number	Date into service	Type	Body length	Notes
1874 build				
'Midland'	25 January 1874*	Sleeper	51ft 6in	To Italy 6 June 1874 to 20 June 1877. Loaned to GNR 26 April 1879 to 10 July 1879. Name removed and renumbered 21 in March 1888.
'Excelsior'	15 February 1874*	Sleeper	51ft 6in	Name removed and renumbered 20 in March 1888.
'Victoria'	21 March 1874*	Parlour	51ft 6in	Transferred to London & South Western Railway, 1880.
'Enterprise'	1 June 1874	Sleeper	51ft 6in	Destroyed by fire at Hunslet, Leeds, 29 October 1882
'Britannia'	1 June 1874	Parlour	51ft 6in	Rebuilt as hotel car 'Windsor' July 1882. Name removed and renumbered 15 by March 1888.
'Leo'	1 June 1874	Parlour	51ft 6in	Rebuilt as hotel car 'Delmonico' April 1882. Name removed and renumbered 14 by March 1888.
1	1 June 1874	Brake parlour third	50ft 8in	
2	1 June 1874	Brake parlour third	50ft 8in	

*Date completed. Into service 1 June 1874.

Original Name or Number	Date into service	Type	Body length	Notes
3	1 June 1874	Brake parlour third	50ft 8in	Renumbered 19 by March 1888.
4	1 June 1874	Brake parlour third	50ft 8in	Rebuilt as dining car 18 by December 1884.
5	1 June 1874	First/second composite	50ft 4in	Rebuilt as dining car 17 by October 1884.
6	1 June 1874	First/second composite	50ft 4in	Rebuilt as dining car 'London' by July 1884.
7	1 June 1874	First/second composite	50ft 4in	
8	1 June 1874	First/second composite	50ft 4in	
1875 build				
'Princess'	17 June 1875	Sleeper	52ft 0in	Name removed and renumbered 23 in March 1888.
'St George'	28 June 1875	Sleeper	52ft 0in	Name removed and renumbered 22 in March 1888.
'Jupiter'	23 August 1875	Parlour	52ft 0in	Transferred to London, Chatham & Dover Railway May 1882 and then to LB&SCR August 1884.
'Saturn'	10 September 1875	Parlour	52ft 0in	Name removed and renumbered 1 by March 1888.
'Transit'	13 October 1875	Sleeper	52ft 0in	Name removed and renumbered 24 in March 1888.
'Ocean'	1875	Sleeper	52ft 0in	Delivered direct to Great Northern Railway arranged as day car.
'Mars'	26 October 1875	Sleeper	52ft 0in	Delivered direct to London, Brighton & South Coast Railway.
'Ohio'	1875	Parlour	52ft 0in	Delivered direct to Great Northern Railway. Rebuilt as dining car 'Prince of Wales' at Derby 1878-9.
'Saxon'	4 February 1876	Sleeper	52ft 0in	Name removed and renumbered 25 in March 1888.
1876 build				
'Mercury'	28 April 1876	Parlour	52ft 0in	Name removed and renumbered 3 by March 1888.
'Juno'	28 April 1876	Parlour	52ft 0in	Name removed and renumbered 2 by March 1888.
'Castalia'	28 April 1876	Sleeper	52ft 0in	Transferred to Italy, spring 1883.
'Scotia'	28April 1876	Sleeper	52ft 0in	Name removed and numbered 26 by March 1888.
'Venus'	3 May 1876	Parlour		

76

Name	Date	Type	Length	Notes
'Norman'	2 June 1876	Sleeper	52ft 0in	Name removed and numbered 27 in March 1888.
'Australia'	20 June 1876	Sleeper	52ft 0in	Transferred to Italy, Spring 1883.
'Vesta'	28 July 1876	Parlour	52ft 0in	Name removed and renumbered 6 by March 1888.
'Minerva'	28 July 1876	Parlour	52ft 0in	Name removed and renumbered 5 by March 1888.
'India'	28 July 1876	Sleeper	52ft 0in	Transferred to Great Northern Railway August 1878.
'Germania'	26 August 1876	Sleeper	52ft 0in	Transferred to Great Northern Railway August 1878 (later to Italy, 1880).
'Planet'	27 September 1876	Parlour	52ft 0in	Name removed and renumbered 7 by March 1888.
'Albion'	9 October 1876	Parlour	52ft 0in	Name removed and renumbered 8 by March 1888.
'Comet'	31 October 1876	Parlour	52ft 0in	Name removed and renumbered 9 by March 1888.
'Ariel'	31 October 1876	Parlour	52ft 0in	Transferred to London, Brighton & South Coast Railway 1 December 1881 and renamed 'Louise'.
'Apollo'	19 January 1877	Parlour	52ft 0in	Name removed and renumbered 10 by March 1888.
'Adonis'	19 January 1877	Parlour	52ft 0in	Transferred to London, Brighton & South Coast Railway 1 December 1881 and renamed 'Victoria'.

1877 build

Name	Date	Type	Length	Notes
'Aurora'	1 May 1877	Parlour	52ft 0in	Name removed and renumbered 11 by March 1888.
'Ceres'	1 May 1877	Parlour	52ft 0in	Transferred to London, Brighton & South Coast Railway late 1881 and renamed 'Maud'.
'Eclipse'	10 July 1877	Parlour	52ft 0in	Name removed and renumbered 13 by March 1888.
'Alexandra' (I)	10 July 1877	Parlour	52ft 0in	Name removed and renumbered 12 by March 1888.
'Alexandra' (II)	10 October 1877	Parlour	52ft 0in	Delivered direct to LBSCR 10 October 1877.
'Albert Edward'	10 October 1877	Parlour	52ft 0in	Delivered direct to LBSCR 10 October 1877.
'Globe'	29 June 1878	Parlour	52ft 0in	Delivered direct to LBSCR 29 June 1878. Renamed 'Beatrice'. First with electric lighting.

Original Name or Number	Date into service	Type	Body length	Notes
1880 build				
'Columba'	1880	Sleeper	50ft 6in	Delivered direct to GNR 1880.
'Iona'	1880	Sleeper	50ft 6in	Delivered direct to GNR 1880.
1882 build				
'St Andrew'	1 February 1883	Sleeper	50ft 6in	Name removed and renumbered 28 in March 1888.
'St Mungo'	1 February 1883	Sleeper	50ft 6in	Name removed and renumbered 29 in March 1888.
'Balmoral'	2 January 1883	Sleeper	36ft 3in	Delivered direct to Great Northern Railway 2 January 1883. Transferred to the Highland Railway in 1885.
'Culross'	2 January 1883	Sleeper	36ft 3in	Delivered direct to Great Northern Railway 2 January 1883. Transferred to the Highland Railway in 1885 and renamed 'Dubrobin'.
1883 build				
'St Louis'	30 June 1883	Sleeper	36ft 3in	Name removed and numbered 30 in March 1888.
'St Denis'	30 June 1883	Sleeper	36ft 3in	Name removed and numbered 31 in March 1888.
'Missouri'	February 1884	Sleeper	49ft 3in	Replacement for 'Enterprise' completed September 1883. Name removed and numbered 32 in March 1888.
'Michigan'	May 1886	Sleeper	49ft 3in	Completed August 1883. In store until May 1886 at Derby. Name removed and numbered 33 in March 1888.
1900 build				
34	April 1900	Sleeper	59ft 10¼in	Renumbered 2771 (LMS) 1 January 1923, renumbered 02771 (1925).
35	April 1900	Sleeper	59ft 10¼in	Scrapped c1922.
36	April 1900	Sleeper	59ft 10¼in	Renumbered 2772 (LMS) 1 January 1923, renumbered 02772 (1925).
37	April 1900	Sleeper	59ft 10¼in	Renumbered 2773 (LMS) 1 January 1923, renumbered 02773 (1925).

The grounded body of a third class baggage car which served as a mess hut and office at Bedford behind the down main platform curtain wall. It is seen here on 12 October 1935 and was broken up in 1966. *R. G. Jarvis*

2 Table of Pullman cars in Midland service 1874-1888

Year	Sleeping			Parlour			Dining			Total		Notes
	New	Delete	Total	New	Delete	Total	New	Delete	Total	Add/Delete	Total	
1874	2	—	2	3	—	3	—	—	—	+5	5+8	'Midland' built but on loan. Also 8 day cars built.
1875	4	—	6	2	—	5	—	—	—	+6	11+8	
1876	6	—	12	11	—	16	—	—	—	+17	28+8	
1877	1	—	13	4	—	20	—	—	—	+5	33+8	
1878	—	2	11	—	—	20	—	—	—	-2	31+8	'India' and 'Germania' to GNR.
1879	—	—	11	—	—	20	—	—	—	—	31+8	
1880	—	—	11	—	1	19	—	—	—	-1	30+8	'Victoria' to LSWR.
1881	—	—	11	—	3	16	—	—	—	-3	27+8	'Ariel', 'Adonis' and 'Ceres' to LBSCR.
1882	2	1	12	—	3	13	2	—	2	+4	27+8	Parlour cars 'Britannia' and 'Leo' remodelled as diners. 'Enterprise' burnt out (sleeper). 'Jupiter' (pc) to LCDR.
										-4		
1883	2	2	12	—	—	13	—	—	2	+2	27×8	'Castalia' and 'Australia' to Italy.
										-2		
1884	1	—	13	—	—	13	3	—	5	+4	31+5	Day car 8 rebuilt as diner 'London', 7 as diner 17, 6 as diner 18.
1885	—	—	13	—	—	13	—	—	5	—	31+5	
1886	1	—	14	—	—	13	—	—	5	+1	32+5	
1887	—	—	14	—	—	13	—	—	5	—	32+5	
1888	—	—	14	—	—	13	—	—	5	—	32+5	

Total Pullman cars December 1888=37 (including five Midland day cars).

3 Subsequent history of cars built at Derby and used on other lines

Original name	Date into service	Notes
'Victoria' (parlour)	21 March 1874	Transferred to London & South Western Railway in 1880 and renamed 'Alexandra' after remodelling at Derby. Further rebuilt at Brighton for use on the London Brighton & South Coast Railway in November 1890 and renamed 'Queen'. Rebuilt again at Longhedge for LB&SCR in November 1920. Condemned 31 December 1932.
'Jupiter' (Pull 72) (Parlour)	23 August 1875	Transferred to London, Chatham & Dover Railway in May 1882 and then to London, Brighton & South Coast Railway in August, 1884. Rebuilt with enclosed vestibules and seating 28 c1890. Became No 1 third class in 1915. Condemned 31 December 1932.
'Ocean' (Sleeper)	1875	Delivered direct to the Great Northern Railway arranged as a day car. Transferred to Italy in 1880 to work on the 'Indian Mail'. Sold to CIWL* 1888, and numbered 216-221 range.
'Mars' (Sleeper)	26 October 1875	Delivered direct to London, Brighton & South Coast Railway with seating arranged for day use. Withdrawn in April 1884 and sent to Italy. Sold to CIWL 1888 and numbered 216-221 range.
'Ohio' (Parlour)	1875	Delivered direct to Great Northern Railway. Returned to Derby in 1878 for rebuilding as dining car and renamed 'Prince of Wales'. Put into service 1 November 1879 London-Leeds. Purchased outright from PPCCo on 8 June 1885 and numbered 2297. Withdrawn from service 1901.

*Compagnie Internationale des Wagons Lits.

Original name	Date into service	Notes
'Castalia' (Sleeper)	28 April 1876	Transferred to Italy in the spring of 1883. Burnt out at Riace on 24 November 1884.
'Australia' (Sleeper)	20 June 1876	Transferred to Italy in the spring of 1883. Sold to CIWL in 1888 and numbered 201.
'India' (Sleeper)	28 July 1876	Transferred to Great Northern Railway August 1878. Wrecked in the Thirsk collision on 2 November 1892.
'Germania' (Sleeper)	26 August 1876	Transferred to Great Northern Railway August 1878. Transferred to Italy 1880. Sold to CIWL in 1888 and numbered 202.
'Ariel' (Parlour)	31 October 1876	Transferred to London, Brighton & South Coast Railway 1 December 1881 and renamed 'Louise' following rebuilding at Derby to a brake parlour in November 1881. Reverted to full parlour car in 1889. Converted to kitchen car 1912. Condemned 31 December 1929 and became a bungalow at Selsey.
'Adonis' (Parlour)	19 January 1877	Transferred to London, Brighton & South Coast Railway 1 December 1881 and renamed 'Victoria' following rebuilding at Derby to a kitchen car in November 1881. Reverted to full parlour car 1889. Converted to No 2 third class in 1915 as kitchen car. Condemned 1932.
'Ceres' (Parlour)	1 May 1877	Transferred to London, Brighton & South Coast Railway 1 December 1881 and renamed 'Maud' following rebuilding at Derby to brake parlour with electric lighting in November, 1881. Rebuilt as dining car 1884. Scrapped after Wivelsfield collision of 23 December 1899.
'Alexandra' (II) (Parlour) (Pull 74)	10 October 1877	Delivered new to London, Brighton & South Coast Railway. Became No 3 third class as a kitchen car in 1915. Condemned in 1932.
'Albert Edward' (Parlour) (Pull 75)	10 October 1877	Delivered new to London, Brighton & South Coast Railway. Became No 4 third class as a kitchen car in 1915. Condemned in 1932.

Name	Date	Description
'Globe'	November 1877	Delivered new to London, Brighton & South Coast Railway on 29 June 1878. Rebuilt at Derby as a drawing room car with electric lighting (the first railway vehicle to be so fitted) in November 1881 and renamed 'Beatrice'. First ran with lights on 14 October 1881. Rebuilt at Brighton with enclosed vestibules c1890. Damaged in collision at Lover's Walk sidings, Brighton and withdrawn in 1918.
'Columba' (Sleeper)	1880	Delivered new to the Great Northern Railway for running on East Coast main line. Sold to GNR&NER as part of East Coast Joint Stock 1 January 1895 and became number 233. Converted to refreshment car by North Eastern Railway as No 2966 in 1902. Withdrawn on 3 November 1910.
'Iona' (Sleeper)	1880	Delivered new to the Great Northern Railway for running on the East Coast main line. Damaged in the Northallerton collision on 4 October 1894 but repaired. sold to GNR&NER as part of East Coast Joint Stock 1 January 1895 and became number 232. Became GNR number 2992 and converted to a dining car in 1902. Condemned on 27 October 1925. Body used as Railway Mutual Improvement Classroom at Lincoln for the LNER. Broken up c1970.
'Balmoral' (Sleeper)	2 January 1883	Delivered new to Great Northern Railway. Transferred to the Highland Railway in 1885 and used on Inverness to Perth trains. (These trains extended to run to and from Glasgow from 7 March 1904.) Used as spare car from 1907 but still in use, June 1911. In store c1918. Purchased with 'Culross' by Mr F. Marks and became a bungalow at Seaford, Sussex.
'Culross' (Sleeper)	2 January 1883	Delivered new to Great Northern Railway. Transferred to Highland Railway in 1885 and used on Inverness to Perth trains as renamed 'Dunrobin' (these trains were extended to and from Glasgow from 7 March 1904). Taken out of regular use and made spare with 'Balmoral' from 1907. Still in occasional use June 1911. In store c1918. Purchased with 'Balmoral' by Mr F. Marks and became a bungalow at Seaford, Sussex.

4 Dimensions of vehicle types

Over ht	Car group	Date	Body length	Body width	Overall length	Bogie crs	Bogie w/b	Weight tare	Accommodation
	Sleepers								
	'Midland'	1874	51ft 6in	8ft 9in	58ft 6in	36ft 9in	6ft 6in	21ton 10cwt	As built 38 seats / 30 berths / Standardised to 42 seats
12ft 11in	'Excelsior'	1874	51ft 6in	8ft 9in	58ft 6in	39ft 0in	6ft 6in		22 berths June 1877
	'Enterprise'	1874	51ft 6in	8ft 9in	58ft 6in	39ft 0in	6ft 6in		42 seats, 22 berths
	'Princess'	1875	52ft 0in	8ft 9in		37ft 3in	8ft 0in		42 seats, 22 berths
	'Columba'	1880	50ft 6in	8ft 9in	56ft 9in	35ft 0in	8ft 0in	25ton 11½cwt	42 seats, 22 berths
	'St Andrew'	1882	50ft 6in	8ft 9in		36ft 1in	8ft 0in		20 third seats as diner
	'Balmoral'	1882	36ft 3in	8ft 9in		22ft 0in	8ft 0in		
	'Missouri'	1883	49ft 3in	8ft 9in					16 seats/berths
	34-37	1900	59ft 10¼in	8ft 6in	63ft 7¾in	40ft 0in	12ft 6in (6 wh)	34ton 13½cwt	As built 1 double+7 single berths
	Parlour								
12ft 11in	'Victoria'	1874	51ft 6in	8ft 9in	58ft 6in	39ft 0in	6ft 6in	21ton	25 seats (27 originally proposed)
	'Jupiter'	1875	52ft 0in	8ft 9in	58ft 6in	39ft 0in	8ft 0in	21ton	As built
	'Ohio'	1875	52ft 0in	8ft 9in	58ft 6in	39ft 0in	8ft 0in	21ton / 22ton	As 'Prince of Wales' / 20 seats

Day Cars								
1-4 Brake 3rd	1874	50ft 8in	8ft 9in	57ft 1in	36ft 2in			32 seats third class
5-8 Compo 1st/2nd	1874	50ft 4in	8ft 9in	56ft 9in	32ft 6in			18 seats first class / 32 seats second class
Later Conversions:								
Dining Cars								
'Delmonico', 'Windsor'	1882	51ft 6in	8ft 9in	58ft 6in	36ft 0in (approx)	10ft 6in	27ton plus	21 diners / Conversions from four to six wheeled bogies
'London' (later 16), 17 and 18	1884	50ft 4in	8ft 9in	56ft 9in	32ft 6in			
Autocars								
'Saturn'	etc 1906	52ft 0in	8ft 9in	58ft 5in	37ft 2in	8ft 0in	21ton	46 seats third / 6 seats first

Right:
A fine shot of a Johnson single in action, in this case No 130, as it heads a down express near Mill Hill about 1899. A Pullman sleeping car heads the train.
LGRP (21370) courtesy David & Charles

5 Diagrams of vehicles

Midland Railway

1

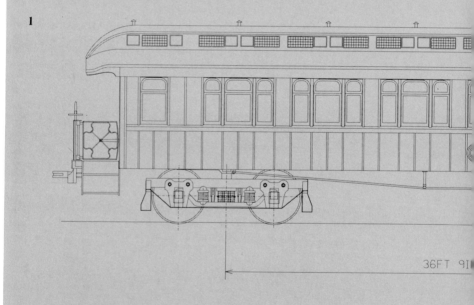

36FT 9I

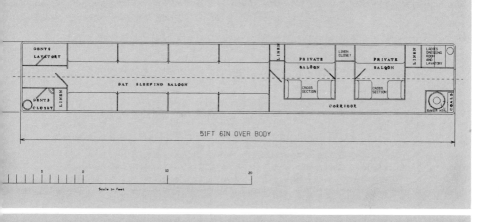

GENTS LAVATORY

DAY SLEEPING SALOON

LINEN

GENTS CLOSET

PRIVATE SALOON

LINEN CLOSET

CROSS SECTION

LINEN

PRIVATE SALOON

CROSS SECTION

CORRIDOR

LINEN

LADIES DRESSING ROOM AND LAVATORY

BAKER MTR.

COALS

51FT 6IN OVER BODY

Scale in feet

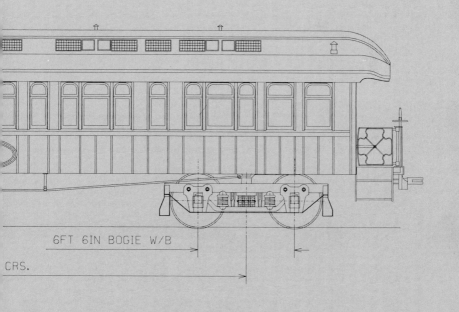

6FT 6IN BOGIE W/B

CRS.

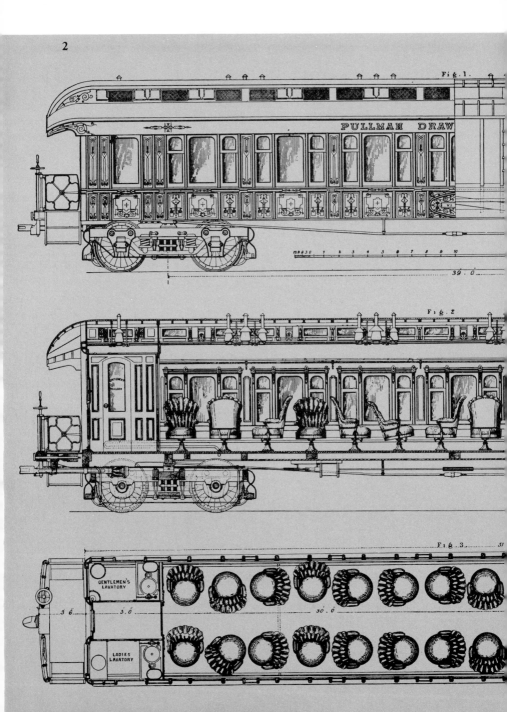

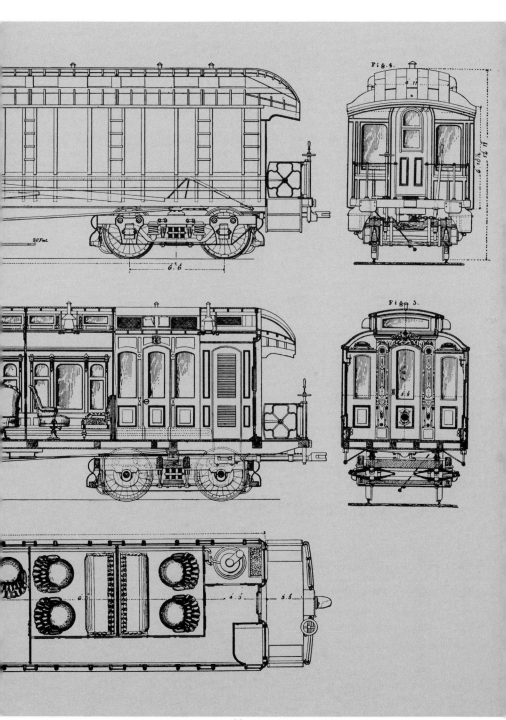

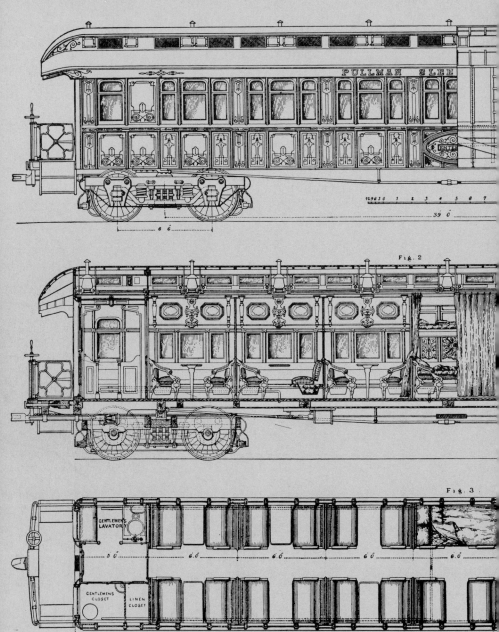

3

PULLMAN SLEE

Fig. 2

Fig. 3

GENTLEMEN'S LAVATORY

GENTLEMENS CLOSET

LINEN CLOSET

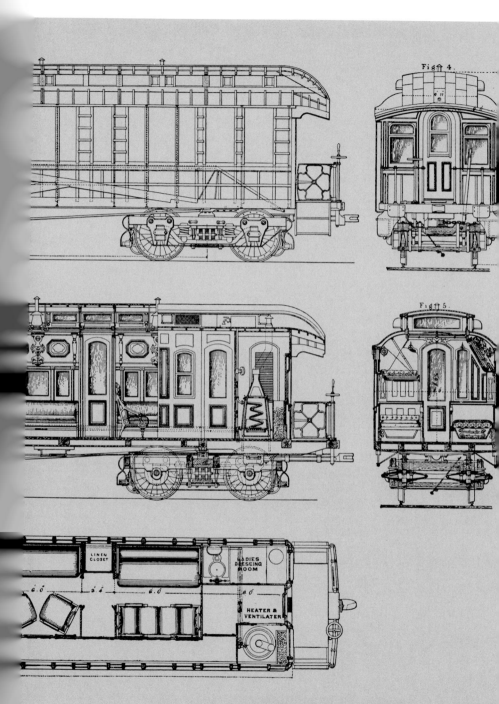

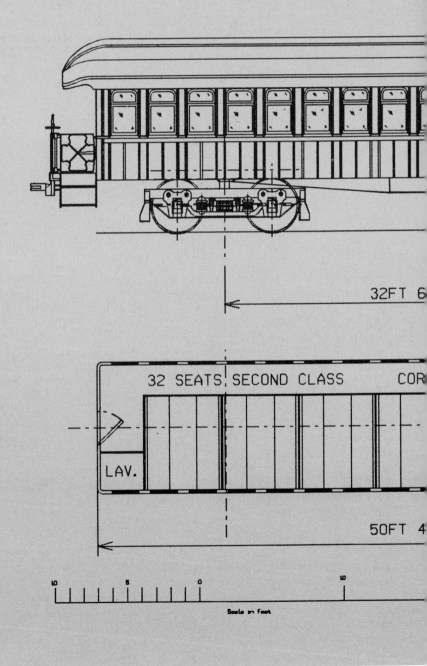

32FT 6

32 SEATS SECOND CLASS   COR

LAV.

50FT 4

Scale in feet

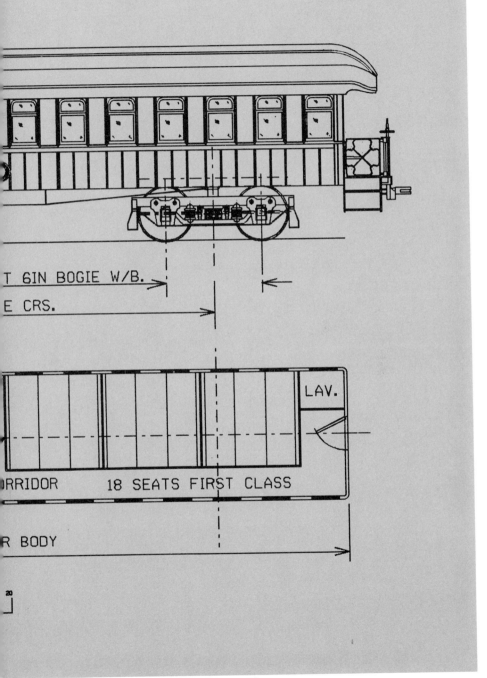

T 6IN BOGIE W/B.

E CRS.

LAV.

RRIDOR   18 SEATS FIRST CLASS

R BODY

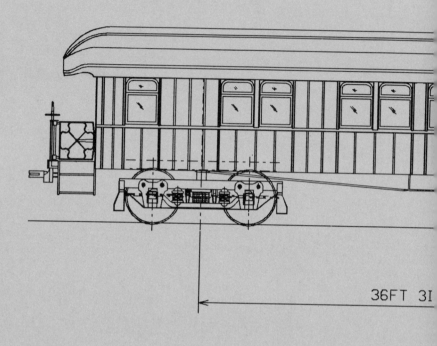

5

36FT 3I

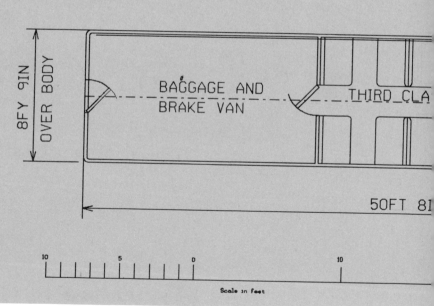

8FY 9IN OVER BODY

BAGGAGE AND
BRAKE VAN

THIRD CLA

50FT 8I

10   5   0   10

Scale in feet

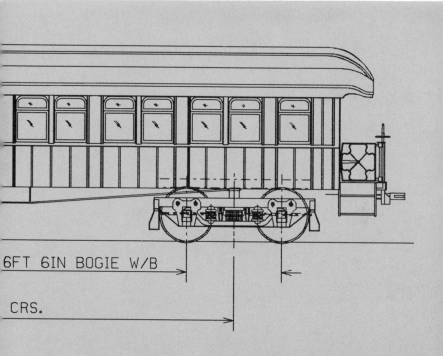

6FT 6IN BOGIE W/B

CRS.

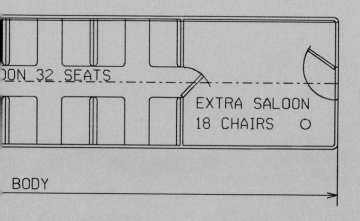

OON 32 SEATS

EXTRA SALOON
18 CHAIRS   O

BODY

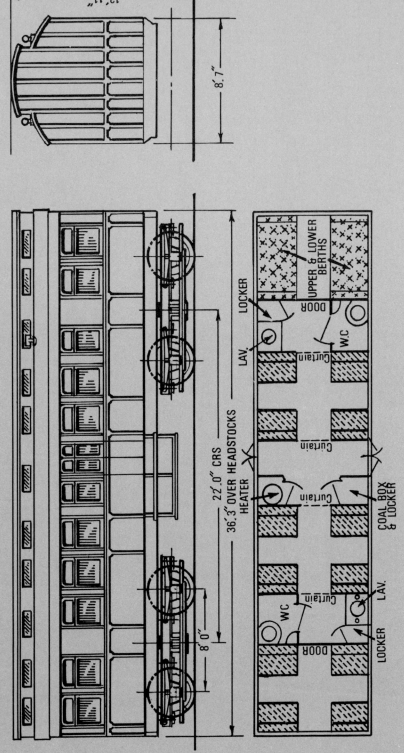

9

12'11"

8'7"

22'0" CRS

36'3" OVER HEADSTOCKS

8'0"

HEATER

LAV. LOCKER

DOOR

UPPER & LOWER BERTHS

W.C

Curtain

Curtain

Curtain

Curtain

COAL BOX & LOCKER

W.C

Curtain

LAV.

DOOR

LOCKER

ENGINE AND PULLMAN CAR FOR MOTOR SERVICE

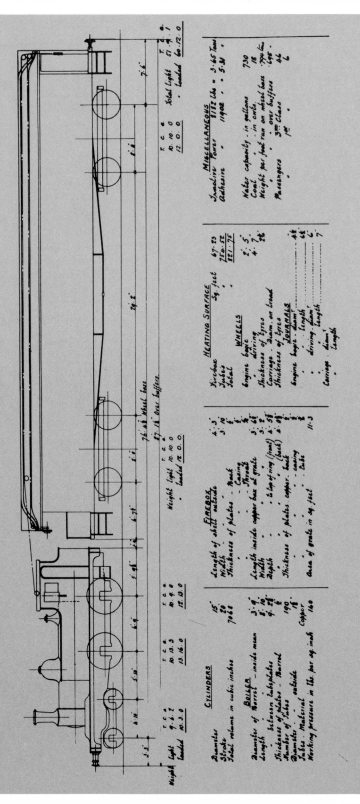

CYLINDERS

Diameter	15"
Stroke	20"
Total volume in cubic inches	7068

BOILER

Diameter of Barrel – inside mean	3' 9"
Length – between tubeplates	8' 10"
Thickness of plates – Barrel	9/16"
Number of tubes	190
Diameter of tubes – outside	1¾"
Tubes – Material	Copper
Working pressure in lbs. per sq. inch	160

FIREBOX

Length of shell outside ... 4' 3"
Width ... 3' 10"
Thickness of plates – Back ... ⅝"
– Casing ... ⅜"
– Throat ... ⅝"
Length inside copper box at grate ... 3' 6½"
Width ... 3' 2"
Depth – ⅜ top of ring (front) ... 4' 5½"
– (back) ... 4' 0½"
Thickness of plates copper – back ... ⅝"
– casing ... ⅜"
– tube ... ⅝"
Area of grate in sq. feet ... 11.3

HEATING SURFACE Sq. feet

Firebox	67.23
Tubes	754.52
Total	821.75

WHEELS

Engine bogie	2' 5"
driving	4' 7"
Thickness of tyres	2¾"
Carriage – Diam. on tread	
Thickness of tyres	

JOURNALS

Engine bogie – diam. ... 4½"
– length ... 6½"
– driving diam. ... 6"
– length ... 7"
Carriage – diam. length ...

MISCELLANEOUS

Tractive Power	5782 lbs = 2.65 Tons
Adhesive	11908 „ = 5.31 „

Water capacity in gallons ... 730
Coal ... in cwts ... 18
Weight per foot run on wheel base ... 790 lbs.
– over buffers ... 690 „
Passengers 3ʳᵈ Class ... 44
1ˢᵗ ... 6

Weight Light | T. C. Q. 9. 6. 2 | T. C. Q. 10. 13. 3 | T. C. Q. 10. 10. 0 | T. C. Q. 10. 10. 0 | T. C. Q. 11. 7. 1
loaded | 10. 3. 0 | 13. 16. 0 | 12. 0. 0 | 12. 0. 0 | 60. 12. 0

Weight Light 10. 10. 0
loaded 12. 0. 0

Total Light 11. 7. 1
loaded 60. 12. 0

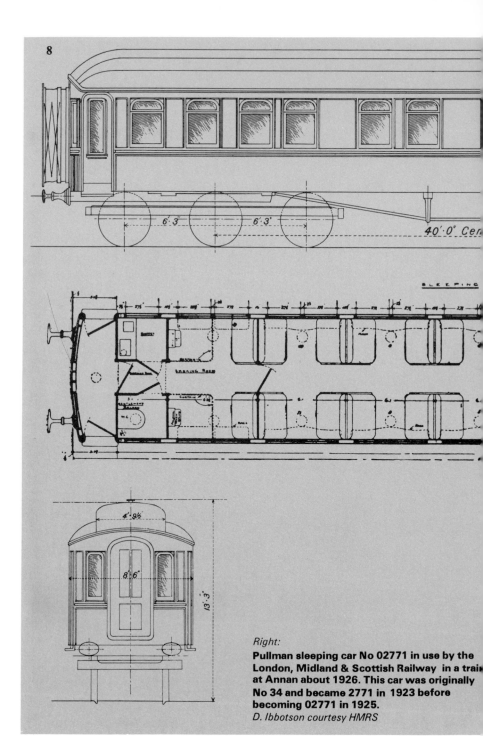

8

6'3" 6'3" 40'·0" Cen

SLEEPING

4'·9½"

8'·6"

13'·3"

Right:

Pullman sleeping car No 02771 in use by the London, Midland & Scottish Railway in a trai at Annan about 1926. This car was originally No 34 and became 2771 in 1923 before becoming 02771 in 1925.
D. Ibbotson courtesy HMRS

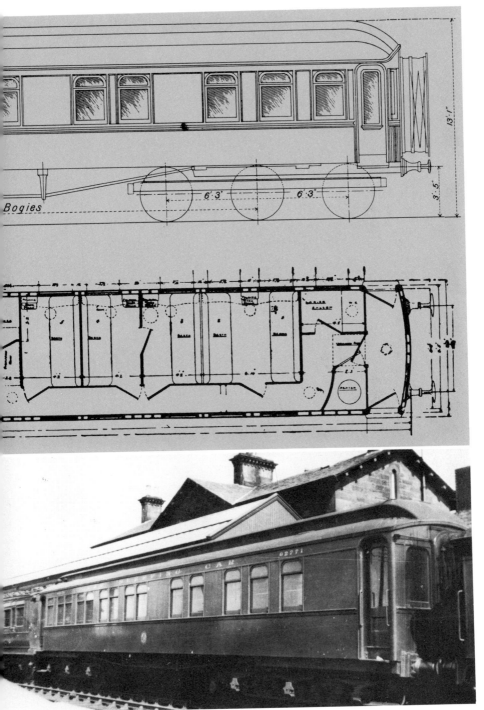

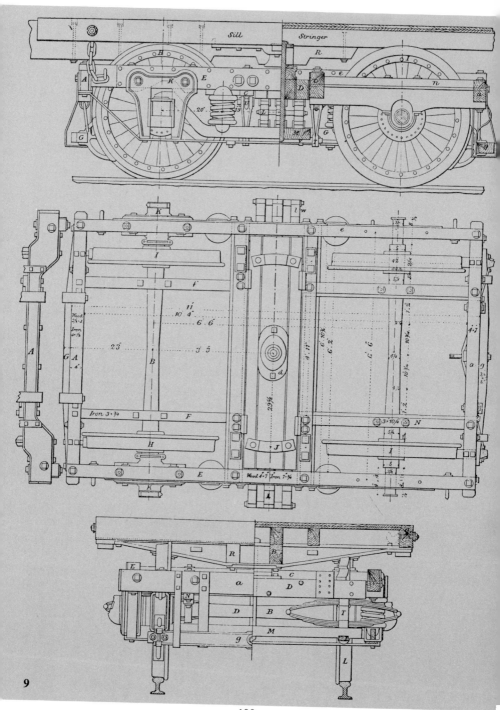

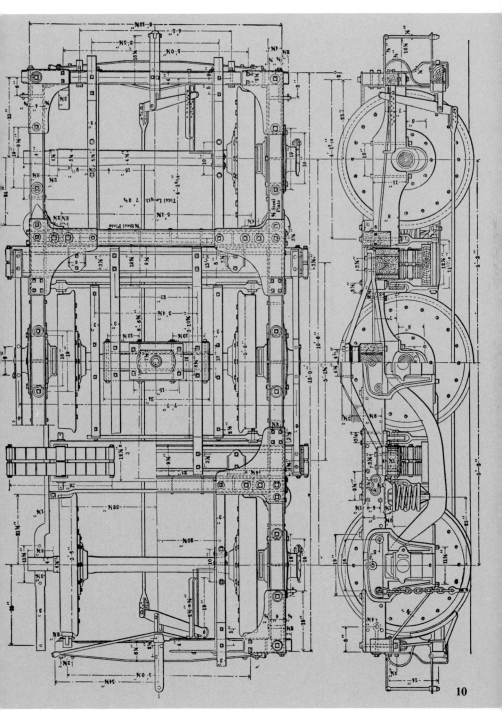

10

Great Northern Railway dining saloon No 2992 built originally at Derby in 1880 as sleeping car 'Iona'. It became part of the East Coast Joint Stock in 1901 as No 232 and was converted to a dining car in 1902, being broken up after use as a Mutual Improvement classroom at Lincoln about 1948.

Crown Copyright Great Northern Railway Official photograph courtesy National Railway Museum

Great Northern Railway (Erected at Derby)

11 Pullman sleeping car 'Columba' of 1880 as rebuilt as a 'refreshment car' by the North Eastern Railway in 1902.

12 Pullman sleeping car 'Iona' of 1880 as rebuilt to a dining saloon by the Great Northern Railway in 1902.

11

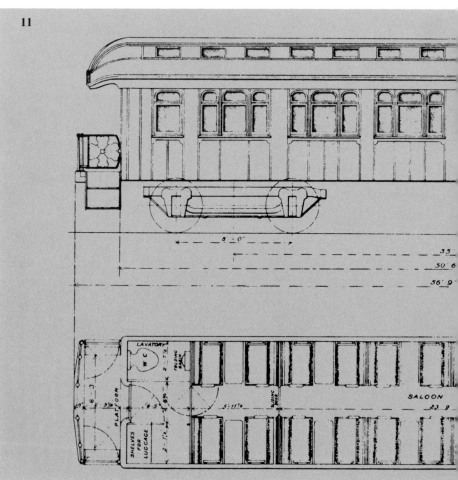

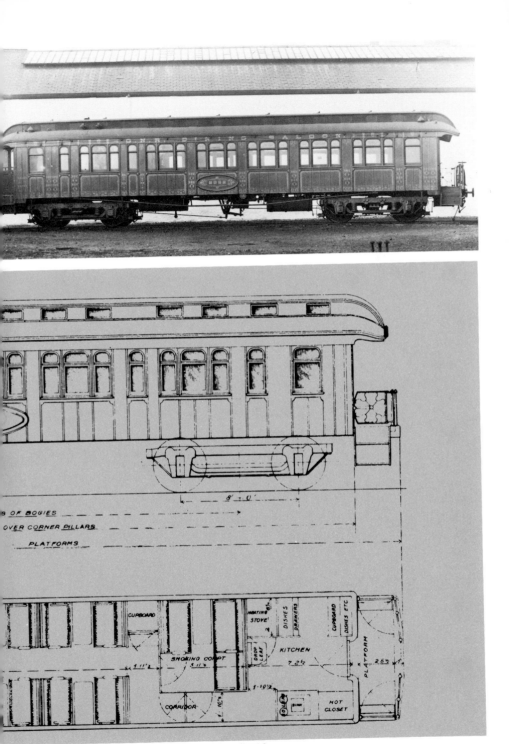

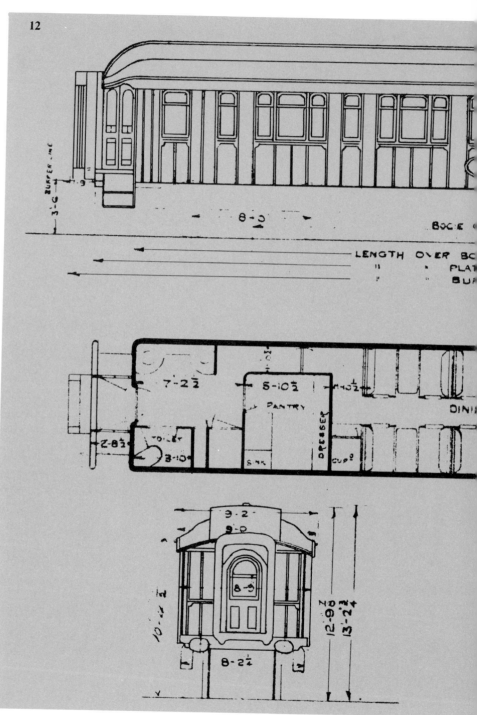

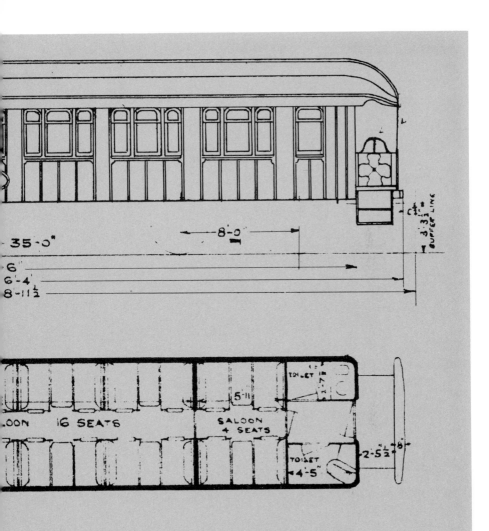

Drawing

13 Details of typical lettering and numbering used on the
Pullman oval centre side panel.

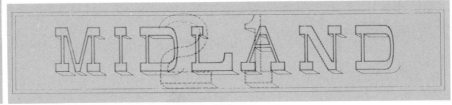

6 The Pullman Palace Car Co Europe - British Operations

General Manager
H. S. Roberts

Secretary (Behrend says General Manager)
-1891   John Miller
1891-1904   J. S. Marks
1904-   Thomas Powell

Mechanical Superintendent, Derby Works
1 October 1878-November 1881   Mr Augustus Rapp
November 1881-February 1888   Mr Joseph Monck
(transferred to Midland Railway Company in February 1888)

Operating Superintendents, Midland Railway Operations
From August 1878 Mr Longstreet and Mr Wildlagen

Principal Foreman, Derby Works
August 1878-November 1881   Mr Joseph Monck

Conductors, Midland Services
1874-December 1888   J. S. Marks
In October 1882   Robert Donaldson
In October 1882   Andrew Baillie

Note: James Bower, who conducted on the 'Prince of Wales' dining car of the Great Northern Railway, is also believed to have been a Midland line conductor in the early years from c1876 to 1879.

Right:
Pullman parlour car body in retirement at Sheffield and serving as a mess hut on 8 July 1959. *John R. Stevens, New York*

7 Reported running defects of Midland Pullman cars

This appendix is included for two reasons. Firstly it details the operating difficulties and delays caused by the Westinghouse Automatic Air Brake and the Saunders & Bolitho's Automatic Vacuum brakes, the first of which was latterly confined to the Midland's 'Scotch' trains via the Settle and Carlisle line, whilst the latter was used on the trains between London (St Pancras) and Manchester and Liverpool.

Secondly it details which Pullman cars were employed and the specific trains in which they ran during the period in question, ie 1880-1887.

Extracts from Continuous Brake Returns
The Railway Returns (Continuous Brakes) Act of 17 June 1878

Date	Train	Delay	Reason/Cause
Half year to 30 June 1880			
Westinghouse Automatic Air Brake			
20 June 1880	12.10am ex-Carlisle	Brake partially inoperative when applied at Skipton, Apperley & Normanton	Air tap at each end of car 'Norman' found shut.
1 February 1880	12.01am ex-London	5min delay	Brake not having been released from car 'Transit' after application at Derby.
20 February 1880	10.30am ex-London	7min delay near Wigston	Brake applying itself. Hose pipe burst on car 'Minerva'.

Date	Train	Delay	Reason/Cause
Saunders & Bolitho's Automatic Vacuum Brake			
28 April 1880	5.00pm ex-London	2min delay in running Bedford to London (sic!)	Springs on brake beam of car 'Albion' require adjusting.
7 May 1880	1.00pm ex-Manchester	11min delay	Brake not releasing properly from car 'Comet'.
23 June 1880	1.00pm ex-Manchester	1min delay Luton	Brake not releasing properly from car 'Comet'.

Half year to 31 December 1880

Westinghouse Automatic Air Brake

Date	Train	Delay	Reason/Cause
20 July 1880	10.35am ex-London	5min delay at Clay Cross after being stopped there by signals	Brake not releasing between compo No 23 and car 'Minerva' causing drawbar hook on 'Minerva' to be broken.
22 July 1880	10.35am ex-London	5min delay at St Pancras	Porter had not opened air tap on main pipe of car 'Saturn'.
28 June 1880	12.12am ex-Carlisle	2min delay at Normanton	Brakes not releasing on car 'Midland'.
12 August 1880	8.00pm ex-London	16min delay between Skipton and Long Preston	Brakes had not released from car 'Excelsior' wheels and blocks of which were very hot.
26 August 1880	1.10pm ex-Carlisle	7min delay near Barron Wood Tunnel	Hosepipe burst on car 'Apollo' and stopping train.
13 September 1880	12.12am ex-Carlisle	13min delay near Cotehill	Hosepipe on car 'Transit' bursting and stopping train.
14 September 1880	1.10pm ex-Carlisle	8min delay at Appleby	Front drawbar hook of van No 3 and rear drawbar hook of car 'Aurora' breaking when driver applied brake.
21 September 1880	12.12am ex-Carlisle	13min delay near Harpenden	Hosepipe burst on car 'Transit' and stopped train.
13 October 1880	9.15am ex-London	5min delay	Leaking hosepipe on car 'Norman'. Pipe changed.

Date	Train	Delay	Description
13 October 1880	1.10pm ex-Carlisle	10min delay nr Cudworth	Hosepipe bursting on car 'Minerva' and stopping train.
26 October 1880	1.00am ex-Carlisle	4min delay nr Sandiacre	Train pipe bursting on car 'Excelsior' and stopping train.
27 October 1880	12.12am ex-Carlisle		Car 'Norman'

Sanders & Bolitho's Vacuum Brake

Date	Train	Delay	Description
5 August 1880	5.00pm ex-London	2min delay Trent	Brake not releasing on car 'Alexandra'.
6 August 1880	10.40am ex-Liverpool	4min delay Marple	Brake not releasing on car 'Alexandra'.
17 August 1880	3.30pm ex-London	11min delay Bedford	Brake not releasing on car 'Comet'.
8 September 1880	4.05pm ex-Liverpool	3min delay Bedford	Defective cylinder, car 'Britannia'.
10 September 1880	10.40pm ex-Liverpool	4min delay in running	Brake block binding car 'St George'.
10 September 1880	12.01am ex-London	10min delay	Brake blocks taken on irregularly, car 'St George'.
26 November 1880	12.10am ex-Liverpool	5min delay	Brake not releasing quickly, car 'Britannia'.

Half year to 30 June 1881

Westinghouse Automatic Air Brake

Date	Train	Delay	Description
1 January 1881	12.10am ex-Carlisle	35min at Doe Hill	Brake stuck on car 'Castalia'.
13 January 1881	12.10am ex-Carlisle	18min near Ampthill	Brake hose burst on car 'Castalia'.
21 January 1881	9.15 ex-London	5min at Bedford	Brake not releasing on car 'Castalia'.
27 January 1881	9.15pm ex-London	10min at Radlett	Brake not releasing on car 'Norman'.
12 March 1881	2.44am from Leicester to London		Brake did not act on car 'Castalia'.
28 March 1881	10.35am ex-London	8min near Woodhouse Mill	Hose burst, car 'Apollo'.
11 April 1881	9.15pm ex-London	2min at Normanton	Hose burst, car 'Excelsior'.
23 April 1881	9.15pm ex-London	5min near and at Kentish Town	Brake binding, car 'Enterprise'.

Date	*Train*	*Delay*	*Reason/Cause*
30 May 1881	9.15pm ex-London	4min at Dent	Pipe coupling between cars 'Transit' and 'Midland' became disconnected and drawbar and screw coupling on front end of bogie composite No 3 and car 'Transit' broke.
11 June 1881	12.10am ex-Carlisle	4min at Trent	Brake not releasing on car 'Transit'.

Saunders & Bolitho's Automatic Vacuum Brake

17 January 1881	12.01am ex-London	1min Luton	Pipe coupling between composites Nos 702 and 64 and car 'Princess' not properly coupled.
8 April 1881	10.30pm ex-Liverpool	3min near Stockport	Pipe coupling between cars 'St George' and 'Saxon' not properly coupled.

Half year to 31 December 1881

Westinghouse Automatic Air Brake

1 July 1881	1.55am ex-Leeds	2min at Hellifield	Difficulty in connecting pipe couplings between car 'Enterprise' and L&Y composite No 236.
10 September 1881	10.35am ex-London	3min in running	Brake sticking on car 'Aurora'.
27 September 1881	8.00pm ex-London	2min at Little Bowden	Coupling valves closed themselves between car 'Enterprise' and NBR composite No 241 through improper position of main pipe on NBR vehicle.
10 November 1881	12.12am ex-Carlisle	3min at Trent	Brakes not acting. Shut valves between 'Castalia' and 'Enterprise'.
19 November 1881	12.12am ex-Carlisle	1min at Trent	Coupling of pipes difficult between 'Midland' and van No 185.

Date	Train	Delay	Remarks
24 November 1881	1.10pm ex-Carlisle	7min at Normanton	Brake could not be released on rear three vehicles 'Saturn' and bogie compos Nos 4 and 8.
13 December 1881	12.12am ex-Carlisle	4min at Trent	Difficult to couple pipes between 'Midland' and G&SW fish van No 27 and van No 492.

Half Year to 30 June 1882
Westinghouse Automatic Air Brake

Date	Train	Delay	Remarks
30 January 1882	12.12am ex-Carlisle	20min at Carlisle	Brake would not release on car 'Transit'.
1 February 1882	12.02am ex-Carlisle	5min at Carlisle	Brake would not release from car 'Transit'.
1 February 1882	12.12am ex-Carlisle	2min at Sheffield	Difficulty in uncoupling hosepipe on car 'Midland'.
14 March 1882	9.15pm ex-London	9min in running	Brake would not release properly from car 'Excelsior'.
18 March 1882	12.12am ex-Carlisle	25min at Carlisle	Brake would not release from car 'Exclesior'.

Half year to 31 December 1882
Westinghouse Automatic Air Brake

Date	Train	Delay	Remarks
3 November 1882	9.15pm ex-London	5min near Carlisle	Brake on car 'Excelsior' would not release after stopping.

Half year to 30 June 1883
Saunders & Bolitho's Automatic Vacuum Brake

Date	Train	Delay	Remarks
9 March 1883	12.00 noon ex-London	1min Kentish Town	Pipe coupling between 'Juno' and bogie carriage No 636 not properly together.

Half Year to 31 December 1883
Westinghouse Automatic Air Brake

Date	Train	Delay	Reason/Cause
22 July 1883	12.02am ex-Carlisle	1min at Heeley	Brake on car 'Midland' not released at Sheffield.
31 July 1883	10.35am ex-London	11min in running Normanton to Skipton	Brake not released on car 'Apollo' through pistons sticking and tyres very hot.
10 August 1883	8.00pm ex-London	12min delay: 4min at Skipton, 8min near Gargrove	Binding leaky hose on car 'Saxon'. Same hose bursting
25 August 1883	1.00am ex-Carlisle	2min near Clay Cross	Brake would not release from car 'St Louis'.
13 October 1883	1.00am ex-Carlisle	1min near Stoney Ford	Brake would not release from car 'St Louis'.

Half year to 30 June 1884
Westinghouse Automatic Air Brake

Date	Train	Delay	Reason/Cause
2 February 1884	12.02am ex-Carlisle	12min, 9min near Hellifield 3min near Sheffield	Train had to be stopped and brake shut off on car 'Missouri' (triple valve sticking).

Half year to 31 December 1884
Westinghouse Automatic Air Brake

Date	Train	Delay	Reason/Cause
16 August 1884	1.00am ex-Carlisle	4min delay at Beauchief	Train had to be stopped to release brake on car 'Excelsior' which had not been released on leaving Sheffield due to triple valve sticking.
31 August 1884	9.15pm ex-London	4min delay running from Kentish Town and 6min delay at Hendon	Train had to be stopped at Hendon, brake had not released from car 'St Mungo', triple valve sticking.

Date	Train	Delay/Location	Remarks
16 September 1884	9.15pm ex-London	8min delay near Sheffield	Train had to be stopped twice through brake not releasing from NBR carriage No 606 and car 'St Louis' owing to triple valve sticking.

Saunders & Bolitho's Automatic Vacuum Brake

Date	Train	Delay/Location	Remarks
31 July 1884	5.00pm ex-London	4min delay at Bedford	Piped not put properly on stop plug of car 'London'.

Half year to 30 June 1885
Westinghouse Automatic Air Brake

Date	Train	Delay/Location	Remarks
30 June 1885	1.10pm ex-Carlisle	5min delay near Barron Wood	Front hose pipe of Pullman car No 10 bursting.
		2min delay near Appleby	Replacing pipe.

Half year to 31 December 1885
Westinghouse Automatic Air Brake

Date	Train	Delay/Location	Remarks
7 August 1885	1.10pm ex-Carlisle	7min delay near Alfreton	Train stopped by front hose pipe of eighth vehicle Pullman car No 1 bursting.
11 August 1885	8.25pm ex-London	16min delay (8min at Clay Cross and 8min at Beauchief)	Train stopped at Beauchief to release brake from car 'St Louis' and MSJS bogie compo No 14 through top spring of driver valve of engine No 60 becoming weak.
18 September 1885	8.25pm ex-London	3min Oakley	Rear hose pipe of sixth vehicle 'St Dennis' (sic) burst.
7 October 1885	12.02am ex-Carlisle	8min Skipton, Normanton and Heeley	Brake would not release from car 'St Louis' and had to be shut off at Heeley where it stopped the train through triple valve sticking.

Date	Train	Delay	Reason/Cause
Half year to 30 June 1886			
Westinghouse Automatic Air Brake			
29 January 1886	9.15am ex-London	1min Leicester	Brake not releasing on car 'St Louis' owing to triple valve sticking.
29 May 1886	12.02am ex-Carlisle	1min Skipton	Brake not releasing on car 'St Denis' owing to triple valve sticking.
9 June 1886	9.15am ex-London	2min running	Brake not releasing on car 'Michigan' owing to triple valve sticking.
21 June 1886	9.15pm ex-London	3min Sandiacre	Brake not releasing on car 'Michigan' owing to triple valve sticking.
Half year to 31 December 1886			
Westinghouse Automatic Air Brake			
9 July 1886	9.15pm ex-London (to Carlisle)	6min Keighley	Brake not releasing on car 'Michigan' owing to triple valve sticking.
14 July 1886	9.15pm ex-London	10min, 7min near Brent and 3min at Bedford attempting to replace pipe	Rear hose pipe bursting on car 'Missouri'. Cooling hot tyres.
28 August 1886	9.15pm ex-London	7min Skipton	Brake not releasing on car 'Michigan', owing to triple valve sticking.
13 September 1886	9.15pm ex-London	17min in running	Triple valve sticking on car 'Michigan'.
21 September 1886	12.08am (duplicate) ex-Carlisle to London	2min Normanton	Front hose pipe burst on car 'St Mungo'.
28 October 1886	1.12am ex-Carlisle to London	16min (six at Scotby and 10 at Keighley replacing hose)	Train stopped by front hose of car 'Transit' bursting.
Half year to 30 June 1887			
Westinghouse Automatic Air Brake			
26 May 1887	12.08am ex-Carlisle to London	2min at Normanton	Sticking triple valve on car 'St Dennis' (sic).

Half year to 31 December 1887

Westinghouse Automatic Air Brake

17 July 1887   9.15pm ex-London to Carlisle   5min Skipton   Sticking triple valve on car 'Michigan'.

Note: After this date there are no further reports in the Continuous Brake Returns relating specifically to Pullman cars.

Right:
1930s period scene at Bath, Queen Square, and behind the lady awaiting a train sits an old Pullman sleeping car body seeing out its last years as office and storage accommodation.
HMRS Collection

8 Journey logs of trains with Pullman cars

Running of the 12.20pm Express from Leicester to Manchester (London Road), 5 July 1878

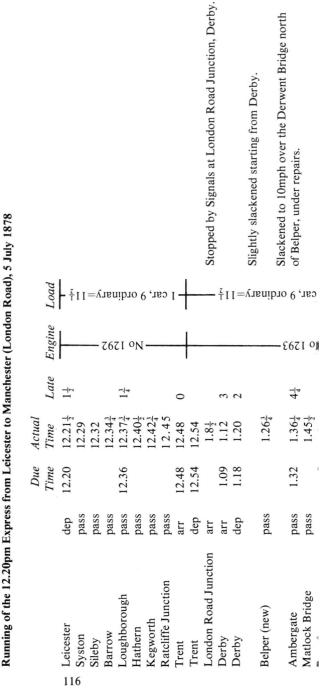

		Due Time	Actual Time	Late	Engine	Load	
Leicester	dep	12.20	12.21½	1½			
Syston	pass		12.29				
Sileby	pass		12.32				
Barrow	pass		12.34¾		No 1292	1 car, 9 ordinary = 11¼	
Loughborough	pass	12.36	12.37¾	1¾			
Hathern	pass		12.40½				
Kegworth	pass		12.42¾				
Ratcliffe Junction	pass		12.45				
Trent	arr	12.48	12.48	0			
Trent	dep	12.54	12.54				
London Road Junction	arr		1.8½				Stopped by Signals at London Road Junction, Derby.
Derby	arr	1.09	1.12	3			
Derby	dep	1.18	1.20	2	No 1293	car, 9 ordinary = 11¼	Slightly slackened starting from Derby.
Belper (new)	pass		1.26¾				
Ambergate	pass	1.32	1.36¼	4¼			Slackened to 10mph over the Derwent Bridge north of Belper, under repairs.
Matlock Bridge	pass		1.45½				

Peak Forest / Manchester section

Station		Actual (due)	Actual	Late
Millers Dale	pass		2.6¼	
Peak Forest station	pass	2.12	2.13½	1½
New Mills	pass		2.25	
Strines	pass	2.25	2.27	2
Marple	arr	2.29	2.30	1
Marple	dep	2.35	2.36¾	1¾
Belle Vue	pass	2.45	2.46	1
Manchester	arr	2.50	2.53½	3½

This train was fitted throughout with **Smith's Vacuum Brake.**
Nos 1292 and 1293 were Johnson 2-4-0s built by Dubs & Co of Glasgow (921/0) in June 1876.

1 car,
6 ord=8½

Delayed 2min outside London Road station.

Running of the 3.30pm express from St Pancras to Leicester on Monday 22 September 1879

Station		Due	Actual	Late
St Pancras	dep	3.30	3.30	0
Camden Road	pass		3.34 nearly	
Kentish Town	arr	3.35	3.35	0
Kentish Town	dep	3.37	3.37	0
Haverstock Hill	pass		3.39¾	
Finchley Road	pass		3.42	
Hendon	pass	3.46	3.47½	1½
St Albans	pass	4.2	4.4*	2
Luton	pass	4.15	4.17	2
Leagrave	pass		4.20	
Flitwick	pass	4.27	4.28¼	1¼
Bedford	arr	4.39	4.39	0
Bedford	dep	4.44	4.45	1
Sharnbrook Summit	pass	4.58	5.1½*	3½
Wellingborough	pass	5.5	5.7⅓	2⅓
Kettering	pass	5.14	5.15½*	1½
Desborough	pass	5.22	5.25	3
Harborough	pass	5.28	5.31	3
Kibworth station	pass		5.38¼	
Kibworth North Box	pass		5.39.30 sec	
Wistow Box	pass		5.40.45	
Glen station	pass		5.41.45	
Newton Box	pass		5.43	
Wigston station	pass (slip)		5.45.50	2 slipped
Knighton South Junction	pass		5.48.20	
Leicester	arr	5.49	5.50¾*	1¾

Engine No 1328, Driver Needham
Load 1 Car, 2 Bogies, 11 Ordinary=17 London to Wigston
                                                 15 Wigston to Leicester

*Slackened over the site of the Hendon accident, over the Sharnbrook Viaduct and through the new station at Kettering.
The engine, tender, 6 carriages and car had Smiths Vacuum Brake.
Engine No 1328 was a Johnson 4-4-0 built by Dubs & Co of Glasgow (1004) in June 1877.

(Extracted from a notebook of Clement E. Stretton in the Stretton Collection, Leicester Libraries)

9 Some notes on Pullman livery and trim

Despite some references to the contrary the following notes are offered as being based on the best possible evidence available.

Livery

So far as can be determined all of the Pullman cars, including the Pullman outline Midland day cars, were finished in the same basic livery as follows:

Body: Dark, almost greenish brown which had an oily appearance. The exceptions to this were the 1900 sleeping cars which were painted in the standard Midland crimson lake, along with some of the Pullman cars later used in the auto-car sets introduced in 1905 which were repainted in crimson lake as well.

Roof: Dark grey, almost black.

Lettering: American style elongated serif in gold leaf, outlined in white and shaded in cream below, angled to the right and shaded to the right in black (see drawing).

Lining: Elaborate gold ornamented 'arabesque' panels of various sizes and designs applied to the body sides, ends and corner body mouldings and to the ends of the clerestory sides. Every separate panel was so embellished.

Trim

Car interiors were panelled in a variety of hardwoods especially American black walnut, with veneers in French knotted walnut and burl and gold decoration. Later dining cars made much use of inlaid mahogany panels with representations of fruit and flowers. Roofs were originally covered with buttoned cloth but later cars from 1880 onwards utilised polished wood panelling as roof linings.

Seats were covered in crimson velvet and claret plush with hand-worked antimacassars on the seat backs. The drawing room car seats were individually mounted on silver-plated pedestals and the ordinary seats had polished hardwood framing and arms.

All metal fittings except the roof lamps were silver-plated. Wilton carpets were laid in all of the aisles and between the seats.

All windows were fitted with tapestry roller blinds.

The seating trim colours on the Midland day cars varied from the Pullman standard being blue for the first class, green for the second class and red for the third class in accordance with the Midland standard of the period.

Index